# Measurement, Guidance, and Program Improvement

*Proceedings of the 1981 ETS Invitational Conference*

William B. Schrader, *Editor*

---

## NEW DIRECTIONS FOR TESTING AND MEASUREMENT

MICHAEL KEAN, *Editor-in-Chief*

Number 13, March 1982

Paperback sourcebooks in
The Jossey-Bass Social and Behavioral Sciences Series

The forty-second ETS Invitational Conference was held at the New York Hilton, New York City, on October 31, 1981. The conference is sponsored by Educational Testing Service. The ideas expressed are those of the authors and do not necessarily represent the views of ETS.

Jossey-Bass Inc., Publishers
San Francisco • Washington • London

*Measurement, Guidance, and Program Improvement*
Number 13, March 1982
William B. Schrader, *Editor*

**New Directions for Testing and Measurement Series**
Michael Kean, *Editor-in-Chief*

**New Directions for Testing and Measurement** is published
quarterly by Jossey-Bass Inc., Publishers. Subscriptions, single-issue
orders, change of address notices, undelivered copies, and other
correspondence should be sent to *New Directions* Subscriptions,
Jossey-Bass Inc., Publishers, 433 California Street, San Francisco,
California 94104.

Editorial correspondence should be sent to the Editor-in-Chief,
Michael Kean, ETS, Evanston, Illinois 60201.

Library of Congress Catalogue Card Number LC 81-48491
International Standard Serial Number ISSN 0271-0609
International Standard Book Number ISBN 87589-927-7

Cover art by Willi Baum
Manufactured in the United States of America

# Ordering Information

The paperback sourcebooks listed below are published quarterly and can be ordered either by subscription or as single copies.

Subscriptions cost $35.00 per year for institutions, agencies, and libraries. Individuals can subscribe at the special rate of $21.00 per year *if payment is by personal check.* (Note that the full rate of $35.00 applies if payment is by institutional check, even if the subscription is designated for an individual.) Standing orders are accepted.

Single copies are available at $7.95 when payment accompanies order, and *all single-copy orders under $25.00 must include payment.* (California, Washington, D.C., New Jersey, and New York residents please include appropriate sales tax.) For billed orders, cost per copy is $7.95 plus postage and handling. (Prices subject to change without notice.)

To ensure correct and prompt delivery, all orders must give either the *name of an individual* or an *official purchase order number.* Please submit your order as follows:

*Subscriptions:* specify series and subscription year.
*Single Copies:* specify sourcebook code and issue number (such as, TM8).

Mail orders for United States and Possessions, Latin America, Canada, Japan, Australia, and New Zealand to:
Jossey-Bass Inc., Publishers
433 California Street
San Francisco, California 94104

Mail orders for all other parts of the world to:
Jossey-Bass Limited
28 Banner Street
London EC1Y 8QE

## New Directions for Testing and Measurement Series
Michael Kean, *Editor-in-Chief*

# Contents

# Introduction

Measurement, guidance, and program improvement are activities that have an admirable record of contributions to educational progress. The program of the 1981 Educational Testing Service Invitational Conference centers on current status and future developments in these three areas. The papers presented at the conference provide convincing evidence that these activities can be expected to help schools and colleges in improving educational quality, in fostering equality of opportunity, in raising educational standards, and in attracting and serving increasingly diverse student bodies.

The relation between testing and equity is examined by Ronald R. Edmonds. He makes it clear that objective, reliable measures of students are valuable but calls for changes in tests and for assessing a school's effectiveness by finding out how well it succeeds in bringing all students up to an acceptable standard. John D. Krumboltz, discussing testing and guidance, foresees that advances in educational technology will facilitate guidance and will lead to a closer integration of testing and learning. In his discussion of the first two chapters, William A. Mehrens raises a number of questions about specific points made by the authors and strongly endorses the closer integration of testing and learning.

Christopher Jencks and James Crouse explain why they believe that changing the name of the widely-used College Board Scholastic Aptitude Test would reduce misunderstanding on the part of examinees and users and why changing its content to place more emphasis on academic achievement would help to increase student motivation. In commenting on their paper, Mr. Edmonds favors changing the test title but not the test content, Mr. Krumboltz shows that the consequences of testing are undoubtedly important but that we know far too little about them, and Mr. Mehrens concludes that the present title seems appropriate and that a shift to an emphasis on school achievement would be less advantageous than the authors think. The issues raised in this discussion certainly deserve further examination.

Lois-ellen Datta tackles the large subject of using tests to improve schools. She describes a number of recent developments that are likely to result in more effective use of achievement tests. She presents an incisive analysis of different interpretations of score declines and suggests ways of making test results more useful to policy makers. K. Patricia Cross gives us an exciting account of what is being done and what needs to be done to develop appropriate educational programs for adult part-time learners and for the individuals she calls "basic skills students." In his discussion

1

of the chapters by Ms. Datta and Ms. Cross, Marshall S. Smith takes a somewhat different, and less optimistic, view of some of their forecasts about changes in schools and colleges. In addition, he expresses concern that changes designed to benefit less advantaged students will receive too little attention.

Significant developments in the identification of talent and in encouraging its development are discussed in the two final chapters. Julian C. Stanley describes progress over the past decade and future plans of innovative programs for academically precocious youth, and points out certain implications of his work for score interpretation and school organization. Progress is also being made in understanding the nature of artistic talent, in identifying promising students, and in developing their artistic abilities. In describing his work in this field, Frank Barron emphasizes the central role of images in research on artistic creativity.

Thelma T. Daley, Arturo Madrid, and William W. Turnball presided at the three sessions of the conference. The ETS Award for Distinguished Service to Measurement was presented to Ledyard R Tucker of the University of Illinois at the luncheon. The committee responsible for planning the program included: Scarvia B. Anderson (chairperson), Charles W. Daves, James R. Deneen, Alice J. Irby, Rex Jackson, Samuel J. Messick, Robert Moulthrop, and William B. Schrader.

I am impressed by the amount of thought, imagination, knowledge, and concern with current educational goals that went into the preparation of these conference papers. These proceedings should be a valuable source of information about current developments in measurement, guidance, and program improvement.

Gregory R. Anrig

*Gregory R. Anrig is president of Educational Testing Service.*

*The citation for the 1981 ETS Award for*
*Distinguished Service to Measurement summarizes*
*Dr. Tucker's contributions through his research,*
*consulting, and computer applications.*

# Citation: Ledyard R Tucker

For over forty years Ledyard Tucker has been developing quantitative models to help us conceptualize problems in new ways. His work is contributing to the solution of both new and standard problems in more elegant ways. Serving for a number of years as L. L. Thurstone's chief assistant in the Psychometric Laboratory at the University of Chicago, Tucker came to appreciate the breadth and interrelatedness of psychometric specialties. He has made fundamental contributions in all of the major areas of psychometrics—especially factor analysis, test theory, scaling, and mathematical models. But the special importance of his work is that it frequently cuts across those areas in seminal fashion.

Tucker's overall impact on the measurement field is not solely in his research. Over the years he has served as patient adviser, consultant, and teacher to a host of students and colleagues whose own subsequent contributions bear the unmistakable hallmark of Tucker's influence. His statistical systems for test analysis have been the backbone of ETS operational procedures for years, and his computer systems for factor analysis and scaling have facilitated innovative applications in a variety of substantive fields.

In the course of his creative and catalytic career, which is creative and catalytic still, Ledyard Tucker has stepped out of Thurstone's shadow to stand by his side as one of the preeminent psychometric theorists of the century. Educational Testing Service is privileged to present its 1981 Award for Distinguished Service to Measurement to Ledyard R Tucker.

**Previous Recipients of the ETS Measurement Award**

1970 E. F. Lindquist

1971 Lee J. Cronbach

1972 Robert L. Thorndike

1973 Oscar K. Buros

1974 J. P. Guilford

1975 Harold Gulliksen

1976 Ralph Winfred Tyler

1977 Anne Anastasi

1978 John C. Flanagan

1979 Robert L. Ebel

1980 John B. Carroll

*From the standpoint of equity, the performance of children from low-income families is the best indicator of effectiveness.*

# Testing and Educational Equity: The Status Quo and Prospects for the Future

*Ronald R. Edmonds*

The task I have set myself is an interpretive discussion of the existing and potential interaction between educational testing and the advance of equity as a charateristic of public schools. I must in fairness begin with the summary observation that the American experiment in public schooling is the most successful occasion of mass education in recorded history. Consistent with much of present practice in educational testing, mine is a normative observation since I compare the United States for these purposes only with large heterogeneous societies of the modern era. Having made that concession to fairness, I must now go on to note that we may also have the most indefensibly inequitable system of schooling among the great nations of the world. I don't feel very aggressive in that assertion, but for purposes of this discussion the proposition is at least worthy of consideration.

We are entitled to be proud of our system of public schooling because there are no problems of race, class, ethnicity, or religion that have not been solved in significant numbers of our schools. It is the existence of such schools that permit searches for school effectiveness to succeed. We must, however, temper our self-congratulation with the

W. Schrader (Ed.). *New Directions for Testing and Measurement: Measurement, Guidance, and Program Improvement*, no. 13. San Francisco: Jossey-Bass, March 1982.

observation that we are thus far unwilling to make all schools as effective as we know some to be.

Perhaps more germane to the topic of this discourse, I am prepared to argue that the present advanced state of educational testing is the most essential ingredient in our identification and analysis of instructionally effective schools. In the absence of reliable, objective measures of achievement, no part of the burgeoning discourse on effective schooling or educator accountability could be sustained.

The interaction between testing and educational equity is the focus of this discussion. I want to begin by defining my standard of equity and by describing the role of testing in that definition. *Educational equity* is here defined as the opportunity for all students to advance to the next level of schooling. Equity does not require that all students engage in such advance, but it does require that all students obtain those minimum bodies of knowledge and sets of skills known to be prerequisite to academic success at the next level of schooling. This means that, while some students may perform better than others, almost no students will fail to master the minima required of the level of schooling to which the student is assigned.

We have already obtained this measure of equity for almost all middle-class students and the overwhelming proportion of working-class students. We are woefully short of such attainment for low-income students, although there do exist individual schools in which the standard obtains. Each of these observations is based on my acceptance of pupil performance on standardized achievement tests as the most accurate and objective measure of pupil mastery of the academic skills that describe the mastery to which I refer.

In fact, because of the confounding nature of class in measures of school effectiveness, I know of no acceptable alternative measure of school effectiveness. I make this observation for two reasons. First, in the absence of standardized measures of pupil performance, school personnel are free to subjectively interpret pupil progress, and that interpretation is often misleading when low-income children are the object of discussion. When standardized tests are the measure of pupil progress, school personnel are denied the easy opportunity to obscure the efficacy of their instructional service for low-income students. Second, school effectiveness is most accurately measured when it is disaggregated by social class. Disaggregation currently depends on standardized measures of achievement. As I observed earlier, our major instructional failings are fixed on low-income children. Thus my measure of educational equity requires knowing the proportion of low-income children demonstrating mastery compared to the proportion of middle-income children demonstrating mastery. In the absence of standardized measures of pupil progress, no such disaggregation is possible. In sum, if there is a methodological message in this discourse, that message is disaggregation first, last, and always.

I want now to briefly survey the status quo in educational testing in the context of the argument that disaggregation is an opportunity for equity waiting to be realized. At the local level, we are now using standardized measures of pupil progress as the basis for program evaluation, student promotion, teacher evaluation, principal evaluation, and criterion descriptions of school effectiveness. Such practices may not be pervasive, but they are characteristic of the most advanced and progressive school practices. At the state level, we are using standardized measures of pupil progress as the basis for state assessment, evaluations of state programs of compensatory education, and programs of teacher and administrator training. At the national level, we have already seen the role of standardized testing in evaluations of Title I and other federal programs. Federal policy analysis of educational equity and the instructional efficacy of desegregation depend on standardized measures of pupil progress.

I regard all these practices as desirable despite the fact that I cannot fully endorse the precise nature of the testing used in these local, state, and federal programs. Later I will describe what I regard as appropriate changes in testing practice at the local, state, and federal level, but for now suffice it to say that the norm-referenced, commercially prepared, standardized achievement tests presently in common use are a distinct improvement over such historically subjective measures of pupil progress as teacher judgment.

I want now to make some summary observtions about the context of my remarks on testing and educational equity. The most pressing and profound problem I see in the American system of public schooling is the failure to prepare most low-income children for subsequent successful access to the next level of schooling. This failure permeates and poisons all our prescriptions for advancing educational equity. It doesn't take a very sophisticated analysis to recognize that in most schools the principal correlate of achievement is pupil family background. That relationship is so strong that you don't have to analyze achievement to be able to fairly reliably predict how well children are going to do in school; all you have to know is something about family background and neighborhood demographic characteristics. The children who have the greatest number of economic advantages do relatively well in school, and the children who have the least number of economic advantages do relatively poorly in school. Breaking this relationship is the outstanding problem that remains in public schools in the United States. Solving that problem requires demonstrating that the relationship between pupil performance and pupil family background is not causal; that is, pupil family background is not the principal determinant of achievement. The principal determinant of achievement is *school response* to pupil family background. Therefore, the problem to be solved is how to organize and administer school districts in ways that cause basic skills to be delivered to and acquired by a much larger proportion of the existing pupil population. It is within this context and the application of tests and testing to assist in the acquisition of basic skills that I analyze the uses and abuses of tests in general and standardized, norm-referenced tests in particular.

My position leads me to make three basic statements about our current testing practices. First, norm-referenced achievement tests can only be defended with the observation that they are in temporary use while we make greater progress in the design of criterion measures. Second, we are probably testing at least twice as much as we need to; it would be educationally sound, and an advance in the name of instructional effectiveness, to reduce by at least 50 percent all the standardized, norm-referenced testing we now do. Third, intelligence testing in schools as it is ordinarily used and understood is probably quite indefensible. There may be some obscure justification for intelligence testing in schools, but so far as I am concerned, there are no circumstances that justify such testing in any public school that I know of in the United States. Intelligence testing is one form of school testing that we could abolish altogether, no matter whether we are talking about children who are in preschool, early primary grades, or about to graduate from high school.

In place of norm-referenced and intelligence testing, what we ought to have in use in schools are locally generated, nationally validated, criterion-referenced achievement measures. I want these tests locally generated so that they measure what is being taught. I want them nationally validated so that the description of mastery in any district is accepted in all districts. And I want these tests to be criterion referenced so that we know for each student whether or not mastery has occurred. Should this situation occur, I would become an even stronger and more aggressive advocate of the uses of testing. If you share my concern with a more equitable distribution of instructional effectiveness, then you can share my enthusiasm for a number of ways in which testing can advance such an outcome.

Pupil performance as measured by standardized achievement tests allows us to describe school district response to the disparate populations attending most school districts of medium or large size. That description is important because the measure of equity with which I began depends on knowing the relationship between pupil social class and probability of access to the next level of schooling. It is especially important to use achievement as the primary basis for describing the local school. When disaggregated descriptions of achievement are the primary basis for measuring school effectiveness, the evaluation of principals becomes easier and much more fair. For example, the principal of a 70 percent middle-class school often has an unearned reputation for effectiveness. An aggregate description of pupil performance may obscure the fact that the 30 percent of the school population that is low income does very poorly. At the same time the principal of a 70 percent low-income school is unfairly regarded as ineffective despite the fact that his 70 percent low-income population may be doing somewhat better than the 30 percent low-income children in the predominantly middle-class school.

My summary point is that disentangling the effects of class and race on achievement requires standardized measures of achievement. Such disentangling is worth doing because the literature on school effects and teacher effects teaches the local school how to make effective instruction available to all children regardless of their class or race. One way to make local schools more interested in the lessons to be learned from that literature is to point out the infrequency with which even most highly touted, predominantly white, middle-class schools offer effective instruction to low-income children. Thus the measure of gain for all becomes our ability to extend mastery to a greater and greater proportion of the school-age population. I know of no instance in which programs of improvement focused on low-income children penalized middle-class children.

My second major area of focus in using tests to advance equity is fixed on individual pupil progress. Parents are entitled to know whether or not their children are learning what they need to know and to be able to do to have successful access to the next level of schooling. Obviously, the most personable way to obtain such information is to ask the teacher.

When parents know their children's teacher to be conscientious, competent, and committed to the educability of all students, then I recommend teacher judgment as the preferred basis for assessing pupil progress. Unfortunately, many teachers don't answer parent questions accurately, especially when describing the progress of low-income children. I must therefore caution parents in general and low-income parents in particular that the standardized achievement test can compel greater candor and accuracy in teacher descriptions of pupil progress. I think it unfortunate that criterion measures are not in greater use since they are far more useful in their description of individual pupil progress than are the norm-referenced commercial tests in such wide use. Fortunately, criterion measures are growing in popularity, and where they exist I extol their potential use for identifying and diagnosing particular learning problems for some students. I think the gains being made in the design, administration, and interpretation of diagnostic tests augur well for the future.

Obviously, I've not exhausted the equity uses to which testing might be put, but I hope I've at least illustrated the point I'm trying to make. In my view low-income school age children have the greatest stake in advancing standardized achievement tests as the primary basis for describing educator effectiveness. Now that I have identified some of the equity uses for tests, what's to prevent our moving at once to implement programs of testing that advance our lofty purposes?

First, most educators have no compelling reason to adopt programs of improvement fixed on the equity interests of their most politically impotent constituents. My definition of equity makes low-income children the focus of analysis and the measure of gain. Such an analysis does in fact advance equity, but is of little moment in schools indifferent to equity. Such indifference exists because low-income families lack the means to either reward or punish school response to their children. The solution to that problem resides in our advancing the old-fashioned but accurate observation that equity interests are indivisible. When schools are made more effective for low-income children, those schools become even more effective for middle-class children. Thus even in schools that meet my standard of equity the achievement gap between social classes remains while the floor of achievement rises for all.

Second, I do not think issues of equity are a pervasive aspect of the psychometric discourse. That being so, the professional discourse on testing is not likely to generate observations designed to advance equity. I'll not pursue that observation because of a recent extraordinary event in the field of testing and measurement. Greg Anrig's professional standing depends in no small measure on the public perception that he is fair, sometimes so aggressively so that he is accused of being a "do-gooder." That he should ascend to the lofty status of president of ETS means we have no way of knowing in what direction the psychometric discourse might now move. Suffice it to say that I wish Greg Anrig well, and, no matter the outcome, I doubt that things psychometric will again be quite what they have been. I'll add that I'm awfully glad that Bill Turnbull is still an important party to the psychometric discourse. It is a tribute to Turnbull's civility that he never conveyed the impression that he wouldn't talk to you if you didn't know what path analysis is. Between them I expect Greg Anrig and Bill Turnbull to make equity a far greater focus of the psychometric discourse than has thus far been the case.

Third, knowledge of the matters at issue here is an area of difficulty. It is barely possible to exaggerate the profundity of public misunderstanding of the nature of testing and its relationship to issues of equity. I recognize that much of the change in testing I've recommended cannot come to pass without local and state willingness to pay for the development of locally generated criterion measures. I urge you to join me in persuading our constituents that investing in advances in local testing practice is a sound, sensible, and efficacious use of the public treasure.

I'll end this reference to obstacles by describing the test maker's most direct role in these matters. To serve the purposes I intend, locally generated, nationally validated criterion measures are ideally produced under the following circumstances. First, a group of parents, teachers, administrators, and other members of the school community are convened and asked the question, what should our students know and be able to do in minimum consequence of their having participated in each of the grades in our schools? As the discussion progresses, the group may emphasize a variety of issues like creativity, civility, or citizenship, but at the core of their description of mastery will be reading, writing, and computation. My major purpose in this description of process is to establish that the summary purposes of schooling must be put forward by those who are intimates of the school. It is inappropriate for test makers to inadvertently determine the purposes of the school.

It may by now be clear that the test maker is not meant to be a party to this discourse until agreement has been reached in defining the standard of pupil mastery at the grade to be assessed. At that point the test maker's role is technical and is focused on the design, administration, and interpretation of measures of pupil mastery. It is a presumption of this discussion that the whole of this process, including the test results, is a matter of public information. This process advances equity to the extent that it describes a school's success or failure in preparing all students for subsequent successful access to the next level of schooling, and we have no way of assessing the standard if the data are not public.

Why does the interaction between social class and pupil performance persist to the detriment of most low-income children? There are, of course, many reasons for our failure to equitably serve low-income children, but two of those reasons seem to me of overriding import. First, most social scientists, including psychometricians, persist in the conclusion that social class is both cause and correlate of achievement. The literature on school effects has not yet replaced the literature on familial effects as the prevailing explanation of the origin of basic skills mastery. For so long as familial effects dominate the discourse on achievement, teachers and administrators will have an intellectual rationale for their social service failures.

The second principal explanation for this failure is political. Most schools serve those they think they must, and when they think they needn't then they don't. Given the nature of American politics, low-income parents can neither reward good service nor punish poor service. That being so, local and state boards of education are seldom moved to action in response to the news that most low-income children are not receiving the quality of instructional service to which they are entitled. This political indifference to the educational welfare of low-income children is surely reinforced by President Reagan's initiatives on behalf of private schooling.

Both the intellectual and the political origins of poor schooling for low-income children can be circumvented by advances in research on effective schools and the testing on which that research depends.

The research on effective schools offers considerable intellectual evidence to those who argue the educability of virtually all children. The frequency and consistency with which schools are found to be effective for low-income children tends to undermine the persuasive power of family background as the principal explanation of why some children do better in school than others. I suspect that the strongest response to the political difficulty is the observation that increased school effectiveness for low-income children almost inevitably raises achievement for middle-class children.

In any case, I am willing to rest our equity prospects for the future on three possibilities. First, the advance of locally generated criterion measures of mastery gives parents and other citizens the data base for the political demand that schools become more responsive to the whole of the population they are obliged to serve. That is already going on in some places, and I expect to see more of it in the future. Second, I believe that most schools want very much to do a better job. Combine that desire with the increasing accuracy and sophistication of measures of pupil progress and there is the opportunity for educators to initiate programs of improvement driven and informed by assessments of pupil performance. Finally, there is the heady prospect of parents, educators, and psychometricians joining forces in support of programs of school improvement.

If the United States can eliminate class as the major correlate of achievement, we then have prospects for educational excellence that are well beyond today's modest references to effectiveness. I think our failure to make greater gains in effectiveness and equity must stunt our capacity for excellence. In any case, I want to close with the observation that a public school system whose credibility derives from its instructional effectiveness for the whole of its pupil population creates a climate of educational discourse unique in American history. I look forward to being a party to that discourse.

*Ronald R. Edmonds is professor of education,*
*Michigan State University.*

*Innovations in testing and guidance can facilitate
learning, can help to develop practical wisdom, and
can clarify students' thinking about careers.*

# Tests and Guidance:
# What Students Need

## John D. Krumboltz

You are about to read one person's view of what students need from
guidance and testing activities, not necessarily what they want or say they
want. When I ask young people what they want most in the future, the
modal response is "I just want to be happy." I can't quarrel with that
goal, but follow-up questions are seldom successful in identifying the
specific conditions or behaviors likely to promote that happiness. The
most frequent request at many counseling centers is, "I'd like to take a test
that will tell me what I should do." Somehow it seems reasonable to
expect that tests and counselors would tell us what we should do. We are
given advice on what to do by politicians, preachers, teachers, and
through advice columns, newspaper editorials, and television commer-
cials. Tests, however, are not designed to tell people what they should do,
and counselors are understandably reluctant to prescribe a single occupational pill that will produce future euphoria.

Americans seem to be less concerned about their children's futures
these days. Watts (1981) recently reported on what Americans talk about
in discussing their personal hopes and fears. In comparing data from
1964, 1974, and 1981, he identified some interesting similarities and differ-

I am indebted to Professor Edward Haertel for a thoughtful critique.

W. Schrader (Ed.). *New Directions for Testing and Measurement: Measurement,
Guidance, and Program Improvement,* no. 13. San Francisco: Jossey-Bass, March 1982.

ences. At all three times the item most often desired was a better or decent standard of living. Aspirations for their children was the second most popular desire in 1964, identified by 35 percent of the respondents. By 1974, it was ranked third and mentioned by only 24 percent of the respondents. In 1981, it was ranked eighth and mentioned by only 8 percent of the respondents. For whatever reasons, Americans seem to be expressing fewer hopes for their children's future.

According to the 1981 Gallup poll reported in the *Phi Delta Kappan* (Gallup, 1981), parents of public school children thought that the three most important objectives that were not receiving enough attention in schools were: (1) developing students' moral and ethical character, (2) teaching students to think, and (3) preparing students who do not go to college for a job or career after graduation. Parents thought that the schools should work harder at developing moral character, thinking ability, and occupational skills.

As presently constituted, testing program offer very little direct help to students in the learning process, though such help may often be stated as one of the objectives. Feedback is delayed. At least a month elapses between administration and score reporting. Even when scores are reported, the students can do little about them. Suppose a student learns that she scores at the 37th percentile in reading comprehension. What can she do about it? By definition there is no way for everyone to be at or above the 50th percentile. The student doesn't know which items she missed, how the scoring was done, and is offered not the slightest clue as to how to improve her reading comprehension.

Testing can be used for a number of purposes. When used for selection purposes, there may be less need to give students immediate feedback about specific test results. ETS fought valiantly against the so-called truth in testing legislation and perhaps lost many a battle because of the clever way in which the legislation was labeled. Who, after all, can be opposed to truth in testing? Perhaps if it had been labeled the "expensive test items giveaway" legislation, the outcome would be different.

But selection is declining in importance as a reason for administering tests. Many colleges are now able to admit everyone who applies. Relatively few colleges are highly selective. Consequently, if testing is to grow and prosper, other purposes must take on greater significance. One of the most important purposes is to aid learning.

With the possible exception of interest inventories, tests are seldom seen by students as having been designed solely for their benefit. Tests may aid administrators to select college applicants. Tests may help school psychologists place students in homogeneous groups. Tests may assist teachers to evaluate their instructional programs. But what good are tests to students?

I would like to suggest three interrelated directions for guidance and testing in the years ahead, directions that are at least partially consistent with needs mentioned by parents surveyed in the Gallup poll and directions that will be seen as clearly benefiting students themselves.

## Integrating Testing and Learning

Testing can be made far more useful in helping students to learn. One constructive step in this direction is the College Board's Career Skills Assessment Program. Testing is more closely integrated with learning in several ways. Answer sheets have been developed so that as soon as the student has completed the test, the layered answer sheets can be torn apart. Students can immediately score their own answers on one part; the other part can be machine scored. Furthermore, an interpretative booklet is provided to explain why each keyed answer is considered preferable to the alternatives. In addition, the booklet provides instruction about ways in which the skills can be learned and practiced, and additional reference materials are suggested. Relatively little attention is given to interpreting a summation of points, although such statistical manipulations can still be performed. However, from the point of view of students who might want to learn how to improve their career skills, the test provides relatively fast feedback about correct answers, gives rationales for each answer, and presents text material to illustrate how the skills can be applied in practice. All this is done within a conventional paper-and-pencil format of multiple choice.

But I am wondering if we can put our creative brains to work to develop even more sophisticated ways of integrating testing and learning. Perhaps you have noticed the increasing number of video games that are available on the marketplace. Arcades that used to feature nothing but pinball machines now feature electronic games. Indeed, the gross revenues from electronic games exceeds that from pinball machines according to a recent estimate. Manufacturers of home video games have had a surge of new business. What exactly are these video games? A wide variety of alternatives are available, but some of the more popular games involve defending one's territory against enemy missiles, escaping from a trap, and destroying space invaders. These video games are nothing more or less than tests. The examinees are faced with problem situations to which they must respond. Their responses are scored for accuracy immediately by impressive displays of lights, images, and sounds. Scores are totaled continuously.

In the counseling literature, we read about test anxiety. One might expect that being faced with these electronic test situations would create high levels of anxiety that people would try to avoid. But strangely enough the opposite occurs. Some young people have become electronic junkies, putting every spare quarter into their favorite video game. People compete with themselves and with each other to see who can achieve the highest score. Endurance contests are held to establish world records of who can play the machines for the greatest number of consecutive hours. Skill in playing the game increases. The constant testing with immediate feedback enables the "examinees" to minimize errors and improve the quality of their responses.

Perhaps the best example of the integration of testing and learning is represented by flight simulators. Jet pilots can learn to meet emergency situations while their responses are diagnosed. If the pilot makes a serious mistake, the simulator "crashes," but no one is hurt and the only damage is to the pilot's self-confidence. Flight simulators are expensive devices, but they cost far less than real airplane crashes. They provide an opportunity for diagnostic assessment of pilot capabilities, but, more importantly, they provide opportunities for pilots to learn how to face emergencies, respond quickly and appropriately, and see the consequences of their actions immediately. We need to develop simulators for many other learning problems, opportunities for people to get feedback about the consequences of different actions and to practice the responses that give them the consequences they desire.

The beginnings of what I am proposing are already here. Toy manufacturers such as Mattel and Milton Bradley are distributing computerized learning aids for reading, spelling, and arithmetic—some that even speak in a simulated human voice. The Children's Television Workshop, which developed "Sesame Street," is now designing software for computerized learning devices. A new journal called *Electronic Learning* is now on the market ("Portents of Future Learning"). Stanford University's School of Education has just launched a new training program for creators of electronic software.

Computer assisted instruction is nothing new, although the hardware is becoming markedly less expensive. The computer can easily provide students with correct answers. What is needed, however, are computer programs that can diagnose errors, offer constructive pointers based on a pattern of responses, and provide practice on a graded series of examples to ensure that students have mastered the concept or skill.

I own a marvelous computerized chess board. It can thoroughly humiliate me if I make the slightest error. It can tell me the move it thinks I should have made. But it can't tell me why I should have made it. It can't point out a strategy that might be more successful. It can't give me a series of similar sample problems to see if I've learned the generalization. It can't do those things now—not at the price I paid for it. But there is no reason that it could not provide a tutoring experience like this some day—if I were willing to pay the price.

An attempt to build a simulation of career decision making with a diagnostic capability has been reported by Krumboltz, Hamel, and Scherba (in press) working with the aid of Richard Kinnier, Stephanie Rude, Lynda Mitchell, and Bruce Peltier. The purpose of our Career Decision Simulation (CDS) was to determine the behaviors that enable people to make better decisions. However, we had no criterion of a good decision. The CDS asked students to select one occupation that they wished to pursue out of twelve fictitious occupations that were available for study. The students had previously recorded their own personal work values. Each occupation was described in such a way that it would provide opportunities to achieve different sets of values. Thus a good decision was defined as one that would yield consequences consistent with the values of the decider. After students had surveyed as much of the occupational information as they wished and had made their choice of an occupation, we could determine quickly the extent to which their choice would give them the values that they said they wanted in an occupation. We used nine of the ten values that Martin Katz and his associates are using in the computerized guidance program called SIGI (System of Interactive Guidance Information). The rationale for the CDS owes much to Katz's (1976) Simulated Occupational Choice, but the actual and operational procedures are quite different.

The diagnostic feature of the CDS seems to have the greatest potential. We could track the path that each student followed in arriving at a decision. Thus we could relate decision behaviors to decision outcomes. A study by Krumboltz and others (in press) revealed some interesting relationships. The absolute amount of time spent working on the problem was not related to the outcome. The absolute amount of information surveyed was not related to the outcome; "double-checking" was also unrelated. However, immediately pursuing more information about those occupations that tentatively match one's personal work values was a behavior that was positively correlated with "good" decision outcomes.

The students who participated in this simulation seemed to enjoy the process, and students recommended it to each other. But the procedure was time consuming and expensive. A simulation administrator could supervise no more than two students at the same time. Two hours had to be scheduled for each student. However, the simulation could be converted to computer administration and probably could be administered for far less money once the necessary programming had been done. Our experience suggested that the simulation was a powerful learning experience. It taught people a method for making career decisions. It showed them how to organize data for each of the alternatives they were considering by the values that they hoped to achieve. It suggested a format in which they could rate the degree to which each alternative satisfied each value. Although it was designed as an assessment device, it may have more value as a teaching tool. Combining both teaching and assessment seems to make the most sense—both economically and educationally.

So let's begin to blur the distinction between assessment and teaching. Let's test in such a way that people learn, and let's teach in such a way that people get immediate feedback about the consequences of their actions. If people see that testing really helps them to improve their skills rather than passes judgment on them, test anxiety may become a thing of the past. Some small steps can be taken with paper-and-pencil instruments similar to those already in existence. The major advance will certainly require the use of sophisticated electronic equipment.

Cost will undoubtedly be a big factor in the development of simulators for educational purposes, but if people are willing to put quarters into machines for a three-minute trial at defending their home from space invaders, maybe they would be willing to put additional quarters into machines to improve their academic and social skills.

One of the arguments against this integration of testing and learning is that it would put testing companies into the curriculum development business. Some testing concerns have felt that they should be independent of curriculum development and provide independent methods for assessing the effectiveness of the curriculum material. If the test builders and the curriculum builders are the same people, it is argued, there will be no independent check on the adequacy of the curriculum. I remain unpersuaded by this argument. The construction of an achievement test is, in fact, an operational definition of a set of educational goals. The testing company selects the educational goals to be measured after surveying a number of alternative goals evident in many curricula. But curriculum builders want the users of their curriculum materials to pass the achievement test. So they must write curricula to match the test objectives. Test builders help formulate educational goals whether they want to or not. Test building and curriculum building are far from independent processes. They are, in fact, intimately related as they should be. I see no essential reason why they should be performed by different organizations, especially if learning could be enhanced by an artful integration.

I am not arguing against summative evaluation in addition to the formative use of tests to guide instruction. Indeed, there are reasons to continue to assess educational outcomes without any direct attempt to promote learning. Tests are constructed for specific purposes. At the moment, I am advocating that one of the most important purposes is to aid students in the learning process. Some beginnings have been made. They need to be extended and improved so that larger and more diverse groups of people can try new responses, get helpful feedback, and practice improved responses to learn the skills they need for their own personal development.

## Testing for (and Teaching) Practical Wisdom

In an as yet unpublished manuscript, Verharen (1981) has suggested that we need to be able to quantify wisdom by developing a "Wisdom Quotient" or WQ test. We have attempted to quantify concepts such as intelligence and creativity but, to my knowledge, we have not yet come up with a wisdom test. Verharen suggests that wise people ought to be knowledgeable in the ways of preserving life, ought to be knowledgeable in the ways of preserving life, ought to know why and how life is to be lived, ought to be autonomous intellectually, politically, and culturally, ought to be able to achieve freedom through self-knowledge, and ought to be able to achieve a degree of happiness consistent with their circumstances. Wisdom includes the ability to give an account of one's knowledge, to teach it, to see when one's own account has gone wrong, and to accept just criticism. In general, wisdom is knowing what one really wants and knowing how to get it. Verharen acknowledges that his definition is abstract and calls for details and examples to be provided by others.

Probably a useful approach would be to use Flanagan's critical incidents technique to identify concrete instances of behavior evidencing wisdom. One of the first persons to apply Flanagan's critical incidents technique was the Old Testament author of the book called I Kings. In Chapter 3, Verse 16, the author begins the familiar story of the two women who came before King Solomon and asked him to decide which one was to be the mother of a disputed child. Let's call one woman Rebecca and the other Martha, although the biblical version leaves them nameless. I will translate freely. Rebecca says to King Solomon, "Martha and I live in the same house. We both gave birth to sons within three days of each other, but one night Martha's child died. She woke up at midnight, took my son from me while I slept, and put her dead child in its place." Then Martha spoke, "Not so, the living child is my son and the dead one is Rebecca's son." Then King Solomon said, "Each of you claims that the living boy is your own and that the dead boy belongs to the other. I'll tell you what let's do, bring me a sword." And so they brought a sword before the King. The King said, "Divide the child in two and give half to Rebecca and the other half to Martha." Martha said, "That's fine with me." But Rebecca said, "No, don't kill the child, give him to Martha instead." Then King Solomon answered and said, "Give the living child to Rebecca and do not kill him, for Rebecca is the mother." And all Israel heard the judgment of the King and saw that the wisdom of God was in him.

Now why does this particular incident provide an example of wisdom? King Solomon was presented with a situation in which he had no basis for knowing which woman was the true claimant; no other witnesses or blood tests were available, but he was asked to settle the dispute.

The woman who protested the king's solution was judged to be the true mother. One of the hallmarks of wisdom is the ability, when faced with a seemingly insoluble problem, to devise a method of obtaining additional evidence or information that might provide a clue to the best resolution.

I personally doubt that wisdom is a single trait. I'm more inclined to believe that wisdom is situation specific and that it can be learned. Instead of developing a solitary WQ test, I recommend that multiple assessment devices and accompanying learning materials be developed to help people manifest wisdom in a variety of practical situations. People are puzzled by innumerable problems in life. They often do not know the wisest course of action. I hesitate to give a list of examples because I have not studied exactly what situations would be most adaptable to the development of tests of practical wisdom, but perhaps a few suggestions could begin a list of possibilities that could then be explored more fully. Here are just a few situations that call for practical wisdom:

1. How should one respond to another's expression of anger—for example, a salesperson responding to an irate phone call from a customer?
2. What is the best way for a person to refuse an unreasonable request from a friend?
3. How do you mediate disputes between two people?
4. How can you tell when rules must be changed—for example, parents changing bedtime for children?
5. How do you elicit willing cooperation from others in a new endeavor?
6. Under what circumstances can you justifiably violate a rule?

Problems in practical wisdom could be devised to cover a variety of interpersonal relationship problems. They could be developed for specific occupations to cover problems of skill as well as ethical and moral dilemmas. Each problem would be complex and would have more than one correct answer. The examinee would have an opportunity to ask questions to gain further information such as is done in assessing medical diagnostic skills. When the examinee proposed a solution, the consequences of that solution would be provided, and the examinee could be asked to judge whether these were the desired consequences.

If designed properly, the assessment procedure would provide feedback about students' task approach skills (Krumboltz, 1979). Students could see their own line of reasoning, the extent to which they sought information, the relevance of the information, and how they organized it. The thinking process could be evaluated as well as the outcome. The entire experience could be extremely instructive and enjoyable if administered under the proper circumstances. It would result not only in some interesting diagnostic data but also in persons who had learned better ways of responding to some common dilemmas.

Bray (1981) has suggested that assessment centers provide an ideal setting within business and industry to determine the extent to which job applicants might fit into a particular organization. Major corporations such as AT&T, IBM, and General Electric have developed assessment centers that include a variety of simulations, games, exercises, and tests to identify talents and qualities useful in business and industry. The notion of developing assessment centers to measure qualities, characteristics, and abilities useful in everyday life is an idea whose time may soon arrive. First, however, we need the assessment instruments and learning materials to stock the shelves. The hardware is already available. Developing the software to exploit this technology is the difficult part that still lies ahead.

## Developing Instruments to Identify (and Correct) Cognitions Leading to Faulty Career Decisions

Within the past decade, behavioral psychologists have discovered that human beings can think as well as behave. Albert Ellis (1962) has long been one who advocated that thinking was the source of emotional disturbances and worked with his clients to remedy their faulty beliefs as well as their behavior. Beck (1976) has identified styles of thinking that cause difficulty in human performance, styles that he labels as distortions of reality, illogical thinking, use of inaccurate premises, dichotomous reasoning, magnification, and arbitrary inference. The approach used by Meichenbaum (1977) has been to teach a set of self-instructions to people who are facing problems they find difficult to control. In all these approaches, the dominant role of cognitions in problem solving is being emphasized. People seem to have a set of private rules that they use to guide themselves in making decisions and solving problems (Krumboltz, in press). Some of these rules are common knowledge, but many are idiosyncratic. We learn them from our own personal experiences and may, in fact, never articulate them until pressed to do so. Even then we may hesitate to acknowledge publicly a rule that we are privately following. Many of these private rules are useful. They are well founded. They may be idiosyncratic but still accurate. However, other private rules may be based upon misconceptions, misperceptions, or overgeneralizations and may lead us to make unfortunate career decisions.

Suppose a young man wishes to become a physician. By chance he is present when someone falls off a ladder and breaks a leg. As he observes the broken bone and the blood oozing from the wound, he becomes sick to his stomach. He then decides that he cannot become a physician. The private rule that he is following, though it may not be articulated by him, might be stated as "I could never help people with broken bones because I would become sick whenever I saw them." He generalizes from one instance to assume that nausea would always strike him at the sight of broken bones. He never considers the possibility that he might learn to overcome this particular reaction. No one tells him that many future physicians have this same reaction when they observe their first medical operation. The young man forecloses a career in medicine on the basis of an untested private rule.

Now here is the problem: How could we devise an instrument to assess the private rules that individuals use to make career decisions? And once we did identify such private rules that seem to interfere with career decision making, what kinds of learning experiences could help to correct these faulty cognitions? The task will be difficult (impossible?) partially because the extent to which people hold private rules in common remains unknown.

Mitchell and Krumboltz (1981) studied the effects of several treatments in helping college students who were unable to make career decisions. Students were interviewed in pairs to identify the types of cognitions that seemed to be interfering with their decision-making processes. A cognitive restructuring treatment was compared with decision-making skills training and a wait-control procedure. In the cognitive restructuring treatment, individuals identified the beliefs that were interfering with their progress in decision making. They were then helped to devise experiences that would enable them to test the accuracy of these beliefs. The cognitive restructuring technique proved to be superior to the other two interventions in reducing anxiety about career decision making and in encouraging exploration of vocations. The cognitive restructuring subjects reported more use of the skills they had learned, were more satisfied with the decision they made, and found the treatment program more useful in making career decisions.

Cognitions that interfere with faulty decision making in college students can be identified through an extensive interview procedure and can be modified through individually tailored learning experiences. Is there some way to capture a procedure like this through tests? Can materials be programmed to help people correct at least some of the most common idiosyncratic misconceptions? Taylor (1981) identified the relative difficulty of a number of career decision-making tasks. Betz and Hackett (1982) have shown that the self-efficacy perceptions of males and females differ in relation to possible career options. People's perceptions of their own abilities to engage in various occupations have a powerful influence on the directions they take. Some of these perceptions are well founded; others are based on faulty evidence and illogical reasoning. Helping people to examine their beliefs, assumptions, and the reasoning by which they make their decisions is crucial. Tests can play a vital role.

## Summary

I have proposed three intertwined ideas of how students could benefit from some innovative work in testing and guidance: (1) Their academic learning could be facilitated by integrating assessment into the curriculum with the aid of advanced technology, (2) their ability to cope with difficult interpersonal and occupational dilemmas could be enhanced by some creative test development in practical wisdom, and (3) their ability to make wise career decisions could be aided by tests that would identify and correct faulty thinking. By working in these directions, we could help the testing service become even more educational.

## References

Beck, A. T. Cognitive Therapy and the Emotional Disorders. New York: International University Press, 1976.

Betz, N. E., and Hackett, G. "The Relationship of Career-Related Self-Efficacy Expectations to Perceived Career Options in College Women and Men." Journal of Counseling Psychology, 1981, 28, 399–410.

Bray, D. W. "The Assessment Center Method." In D. H. Montross and C. J. Shinkman (Eds.), Career Development in the 1980s: Theory and Practice. Springfield, Ill.: Thomas, 1981.

Ellis, A. Reasons and Emotion in Psychotherapy. New York: Stuart, 1962.

Gallup, G. H. "The 13th Annual Gallup Poll of the Public's Attitudes Toward the Public Schools." Phi Delta Kappan, 1981, 63 (1), 33–47.

Katz, M. R. Simulated Occupational Choice: A Measure of Competencies in Career Decision Making. Final Report. Washington, D.C.: National Institute of Education, 1976. ERIC No. ED 121841.

Krumboltz, J. D. "A Social Learning Theory of Career Decision Making." In A. M. Mitchell, G. B. Jones, and J. D. Krumboltz (Eds.), Social Learning and Career Decision Making. Cranston, R. I.: Carroll Press, 1979.

Krumboltz, J. D. Private Rules in Career Decision Making. Columbus: National Center for Research in Vocational Education, Ohio State University, in press.

Krumboltz, J. D., Hamel, D. A., and Scherba, D. S. "Measuring the Quality of Career Decisions." In J. D. Krumbolz and D. A. Hamel (Eds.), Assessing Career Development. Palo Alto, Calif.: Mayfield, in press.

Krumboltz, J. D. and others. Decision-Making Behaviors Associated with "Good" and "Poor" Outcomes in a Simulated Career Decision. Unpublished manuscript. Stanford, Calif.: School of Education, Stanford University.

Meichenbaum, D. Cognitive Behavior Modification. New York: Plenum, 1977.

Mitchell, L. K., and Krumboltz, J. D. "The Effect of Training in Cognitive Restructuring on the Inability to Make Career Decisions." Paper presented at the annual convention of the American Psychological Association, Los Angeles, August 1981.

"Portents of Future Learning." Time, September 21, 1981, p. 65.

Taylor, K. M. "Applications of Self-Efficacy Theory to Career Decision Making and Vocational Indecision in College Women and Men." Paper presented at the annual convention of the American Psychological Association, Los Angeles, August 1981.

Verharen, C. C. *Rationality in Philosophy and Science*. Unpublished manuscript. Washington, D.C.: Department of Philosophy, Howard University.

Watts, W. "American's Hopes and Fears: The Future Can Fend for Itself." *Psychology Today*, 1981, *15* (9), 36–48.

*John D. Krumboltz is professor of education and psychology, Stanford University.*

*Clarifying the meaning of equity in education and
integrating testing and learning are urgent tasks
confronting testers and guidance specialists.*

# Tests and Guidance: Equity and Student Need

*William A. Mehrens*

When I first read the title of Edmond's talk in the printed program,
"Testing and Equity in Educational Public Policy," I was reminded of a
piece Thomas Sowell (1981) wrote recently for *Newsweek*. In it he
discussed the various connotations of the word *equality*. Sowell does not
favor, nor do I, the argument that if outcomes are unequal, the rules must
have been applied unequally. But surely there are many definitions of
equality, and so one must begin with defining terms.

Edmonds has defined *equity* as "the opportunity for all students
to advance to the next level of schooling." This equity would "require
that all students obtain those minimum bodies of knowledge and sets of
skills known to be prerequisite to academic success at the next level of
schooling." This equity should not cause, if achieved, any reduced
variance in the nonminimal objectives. One major problem with
Edmonds's definition is that we do not know what those minimums are.
All the controversy over where and how to set the cutting score on minimum competency tests indicates that. Most score-setting procedures used
for high school graduation minimum competency tests are not based on
known prerequisites for college work. Nor should one infer that acceptable college work is obtainable by a person who passes a high school
competency exam.

W. Schrader (Ed.). *New Directions for Testing and Measurement: Measurement,
Guidance, and Program Improvement*, no. 13. San Francisco: Jossey-Bass, March 1982.

Illustrative of the difficulty one might have deciding minimum prerequisites for college was brought out in the 1979 *Debra P.* case. Expert witnesses for the plaintiffs argued against the requirement of passing the test to receive a diploma on the basis that, since one needs a diploma to enter college, the result would be a 20 percent decline in black students attending college (see footnote 6, p. 50 of *Debra P. v. Turlington*, 1979). Evidently the plaintiffs believed that one did not need to be able to pass a test that was generally considered to cover seventh- and eighth-grade material in order to "succeed" in some colleges. I can visualize such colleges and imagine the experts could find some evidence showing one can graduate from college without having acquired elementary school skills. (That is one reason the public thinks it might be wise to have minimum competency exams for teachers.) In summary, I do not favor definitions of equity based on outcomes and I think Edmonds's definition would be very difficult to operationalize with any degree of consensus.

The terms *norm-referenced tests* (NRTs) and *criterion-referenced tests* (CRTs) suffer from even more diverse meanings than equity. One thrust of Edmonds's chapter is that CRTs will better serve to promote equity than NRTs, which are accepted until we get those better CRTs. Before I comment on that, we need a brief discussion of what those terms mean. When I read the works of different authors on the topic of NRTs and CRTs, I am frequently reminded of the statement by Humpty Dumpty in Carroll's *Through the Looking Glass*. "When I use a word it means just what I choose it to mean—neither more nor less." Actually only two people in the whole world really know what those terms mean—and they adamantly disagree.

Now I surely do not blame Edmonds for the confusion in the literature. (Although I believe he has just contributed to it with the phrase "locally generated, nationally validated, criterion-referenced achievement measures.") Further, I am sure Edmonds knows exactly what he means by those terms—and he means neither more nor less. The problem is I do not know exactly what he means and, I strongly suspect, he uses the terms differently than I do. I, naturally, prefer my connotations. I have written elsewhere at length on the topic (for example, Mehrens and Ebel, 1979; Mehrens and Lehmann, 1978), and I will not reiterate all my views here. We all know the basic differences between norm- and criterion-referenced score interpretation. The first is referenced to a norm group, the second to a specified performance standard. There has been some debate historically about whether the standard meant the identification of the content domain or the setting of a cut-off score (or scores). Current self-appointed experts in CRTs seem to by and large argue for the former. Users probably connote the latter usage due to the close association in their minds between criterion-referenced tests and mastery and minimal competency testing. Edmonds clearly includes the notion of a cut-off score in his usage of the phrase.

Some writers have implied (at least readers have inferred) that norm-referenced tests do not have a specified domain. This makes little sense. If a test does not adequately represent a domain (what for years we called a lack of content validity), it is not because it has norms. The process of norming a test does not have some mystical negative impact on the content validity. CRT advocates admit this and in fact now argue we should norm our CRTs.

I suspect the distinction Ron wishes to make between locally generated criterion-referenced tests and standardized norm-referenced tests has to do with who determines the domain, the degree to which a test represents that domain (that is, is content valid), and the breadth of the domain. I would not use the terms norm-referenced and criterion-referenced to differentiate tests on these dimensions. I have no idea what he means by nationally validated or how we would do that.

All of the preceding seems a fairly long discussion of terms, but without it I feel dialogue would suffer. Let me now turn to some points Edmonds made with which I strongly agree. There are a lot of those; several points seem particularly worthy of reiteration and applause:

1. A principal correlate of achievement is pupil family background. Most psychometricians probably do believe that home environment and quality of parenting do impact upon pupil achievement. (There is considerable evidence and logic supportive of that belief.)

2. We currently do not have equity under Edmonds's definition.

3. Pupil performance on standardized achievement tests is the most accurate and objective measure of pupil mastery of the academic skills.

4. It is useful to disaggregate measures of achievement. It is necessary if we wish to determine how close we are to Edmonds's definition of equity.

5. There is no acceptable *substitute* for the use of tests in judging a school building's instructional effectiveness. (We may wish to *supplement* the test data with other measures.)

6. The core of what parents want from schools is that their children be able to read, to write, and to compute. (I suspect Edmonds believes, as I do, that this is a constant across local settings.)

7. Public participation in the process of establishing the summary purposes of schooling is a good thing.

8. Achievement data should be open to public scrutiny.

9. We should be able to report with some specificity what it is students can do in relation to a set of objectives.

10. Constructing good locally developed criterion-referenced tests is a laborious task.

For all my agreements with Edmonds, he has made some points I question. First, I doubt if we overtest with standardized achievement tests by a factor of two. This is not true in the schools I know about.

Second, I am not as sanguine as Edmonds is that increased efforts to achieve the broader acquisition of basic skills will not result in lesser acquisition by those now at the top of the achievement ladder. If we were to really prepare every high school graduate to be ready to take college mathematics, it would take some considerable reallocation of funds. If total resources are fixed and allocation of resources affects achievement levels, it seems axiomatic that increased efforts on the basics will result in decreased efforts and decreased achievement on other higher-level objectives. I am not suggesting the trade-off is necessarily bad. My belief about that would depend on the *degree* of resource reallocation (we are back to Sowell's treatise on equality). I do believe it important that we at least recognize the high probability that someone suffers educationally when resources get reallocated. Of course, if we can teach the basics better with no additional resources, we obviously should do so. But the labor and cost of those locally constructed, nationally validated tests Edmonds advocates and the resultant remediation of those who fail must take time and resources away from something else.

Third, I believe commercially published, standardized, survey achievement tests that have both normative and objectively based information available are more useful than Edmonds believes them to be for the purposes of equity, which he espouses. My defense is that Edmonds is correct (as I stated earlier) when he suggests that parents want their students to be able to read, write, and compute. These basic objectives are common across communities, and a test that measures reading, writing, and computing in one locality can do so in another. It seems terribly inefficient to the local taxpayers of every community to spend money for the local construction of a high-quality measuring instrument to measure these common objectives. Why not hire outside experts to do the job for the total set of schools better and more cheaply? Those outside experts need not define the domain and dictate it to others. They can build a test covering the domain of basics determined in the public dialogue Edmonds advocates. I do not believe current commercial tests have dictated the domain, and it certainly is not a necessary concomitant to commercial test construction. I believe, in general, that experts can build tests with better content validity (or more closely matched to the domain, or more criterion referenced if you prefer those terms). They can and have built tests covering both broad and narrow domains. Local users always have the option of setting their own cutting score if that is what criterion referencing means.

Before turning my remarks to the second chapter, let me remind the reader that I listed ten points of agreement with Edmonds's remarks while I questioned only three. His chapter makes many points that we as a profession can ponder and discuss in the years to come.

I found the chapter by Krumboltz to be very intellectually stimulating. He has certainly thrown out some challenges to the professionals in testing and guidance. But note that, formidable as those challenges are, he has accepted some of them. He has picked up his own gauntlet. Through his own research, he is struggling toward the somewhat visionary goals he advocates. I admire that. I wish him success. I trust his presentation will result in increased efforts by others toward the kinds of assessment devices he advocates.

Early in his chapter, Krumboltz makes a distinction between what students want and what they need from counselors and tests. I hope in another work at another time Krumboltz will address that point more fully. I agree with his example, but I'm not sure the distinction is always clear. A want can be an unfulfilled need or an objective we should not desire.

Flanagan and Russ-Eft (1975) did a study on what educational experiences contribute toward overall well-being or quality of life: "By far the most important factor inhibiting the personal and educational development of these young people was the failure to assist them in developing goals and plans. Lack of knowledge of their own interest, abilities, and values and the relations of these to the requirements for various types of educational programs and career activities resulted in much wasted time, lack of motivation, and personal frustration" (p. 62).

Now are these conclusions, based on interviews, indicating wants, needs, or both? If they are needs, can we fulfill them with current assessment devices? What proportion of the unfulfilled need can be attributed to instrumentation inadequacies, what proportion to counselor inadequacies, what proportion to the unrealism of the expectation? (Unrealism doesn't turn a need into a want.)

If the conclusions of the survey indicate wants—but not needs (that is, goals we should not be working towards)—how do we convince the public? I believe a current problem with testing is the incorrect and unrealistic expectations of the public that lead to criticism and dissatisfaction when expectations are not met.

I am in no way suggesting that Krumboltz should have given more attention to that topic. He has challenged us quite enough in his chapter. But I do challenge Krumboltz (and the rest of us) to attend more to the wants and needs problem.

Of the three interrelated directions for guidance and testing Krumboltz discussed, I believe we have worked hardest and perhaps proceeded the farthest toward integrating testing and learning. For example, a group of us at Michigan State University has been spending a small amount of taxpayers' money on a project entitled "Integrating Assessment with

Instruction" (Rudman and others, 1981). Our strategy has been to devise a professional development program that should provide skills to teachers on the use of currently available data. Although we are reasonably happy with our results, we realize our approach is indirect. We wish to help teachers make better instructional decisions thereby facilitating student learning. I believe Krumboltz is correct to suggest that to use tests to *directly* facilitate student learning we need more technically sophisticated procedures. However, test publishing companies do much better than Krumboltz suggests with his percentile example. For achievement tests, publishers report and students can be told which items were missed and how the scoring was done. Usually teachers' manuals give instructional suggestions for improving the skills tested.

Nevertheless, publishers can become even more technically sophisticated. The video game approach is a good example. I very much like John's point that video games are nothing more or less than tests, that the "test anxiety" they create serves as a positive not a negative reinforcer, and that people can relish competition with themselves and each other to see who achieves the highest score. We must remember, though, that no terribly important outcome depends on a video game score. If video games or test results assist in important decisions, the anxiety may increase past the optimal level. Also, we need to keep in mind that someone must pay for all the developmental and administrative costs of such video game tests.

I wish I had something wise to say about developing a wisdom quotient or a multiple set of such measures. I doubt very much if I will expend my future professional energies working on such a project. If Krumboltz does, will we not eventually judge who made the wiser decision based on the results? I view this as one of the major problems of measuring wisdom. Wisdom is an after-the-fact inference based on the outcome of a decision. All Israel would not have thought Solomon so wise if both mothers had agreed to Solomon's original suggestion.

I agree with Krumboltz that wisdom is probably not a single trait and that it can be learned (although it is my understanding that Solomon's wisdom was a gift from God). Certainly if we define wisdom as a "task approach skill," it is learnable. But if it is situation specific, I'm not sure how we would build a general wisdom test.

The third interrelated idea Krumboltz mentioned is the developing of instruments to identify and correct cognitions leading to faulty career decisions. Now that seems like a wise idea if it can be done. But Krumboltz refers to idiosyncratic, private rules that individuals use. Discovering these rules and correcting them through a test would be, as he admits, a formidable undertaking.

In conclusion, both Edmonds and Krumboltz have presented very worthy ideas and suggestions that have considerable educational implications. These ideas are deserving of continued professional discussion. I hope my brief remarks can serve as a further catalyst. May we all be wiser.

## References

*Debra P.* vs. *Turlington,* No. 78-892-Civ-T-C (Jacksonville, Fla., July 17, 1979).

Flanagan, J. C., and Russ-Eft, D. *An Empirical Study to Aid in Formulating Educational Goals.* Palo Alto, Calif.: American Institutes for Research, 1975.

Mehrens, W. A., and Ebel, R.L. "Some Comments on Criterion-Referenced and Norm-Referenced Tests." *Measurement in Education,* 1979, *10* (1), 1–8.

Mehrens, W. A., and Lehmann, I. J. *Measurement and Evaluation in Education and Psychology.* (2nd ed.) New York: Holt, Rinehart and Winston, 1978.

Rudman, H. C., and others. "Integrating Assessment with Instruction: A Report." A symposium at the annual meeting of the National Council on Measurement in Education, Los Angeles, April 1981.

Sowell, T. "We're Not Really 'Equal'." *Newsweek,* September 7, 1981, p. 13.

*William A. Mehrens is professor of measurement and evaluation, Michigan State University.*

*Tests used in college admissions should be designed*
*to reward diligence and seriousness during the high*
*school years; the SAT does not appear to do this.*

# Should We Relabel the SAT
# . . . or Replace It?

## Christopher Jencks
## James Crouse

More than 90 percent of all four-year colleges in the United States require applicants to take some kind of academic "aptitude" test. Most require the College Board's Scholastic Aptitude Test (SAT), designed by the Educational Testing Service. Almost all the rest require American College Testing's ACT, which is similar to the SAT but shorter. The first part of our chapter will describe how American colleges, alone among the world's institutions of higher learning, came to emphasize "aptitude" rather than "achievement" tests in their admissions decisions. We will then argue that these tests do not in fact measure "aptitude," at least as most people use that term, and that so-called aptitude tests should be relabeled to make clear that they measure particular forms of achievement—mainly vocabulary, reading comprehension, and abilty to use basic mathematics. We will then compare these so-called aptitude tests to tests that measure achievement in secondary school subjects such as history, literature, science, mathematics, and languages. We will show that the two sorts of tests predict college grades, college completion, and economic success in adulthood equally well and that they pose roughly comparable problems for college applicants from inferior secondary schools and from disadvantaged family backgrounds. We will conclude by arguing that the College

W. Schrader (Ed.). *New Directions for Testing and Measurement: Measurement,*
*Guidance, and Program Improvement,* no. 13. San Francisco: Jossey-Bass, March 1982.

Board and ETS should urge colleges to require all their applicants to take conventional achievement tests in several subjects taught in secondary school, either in addition to the SAT or in place of it, on the grounds that this requirement would have a positive effect both on the quality of secondary education and on the way both students and adults think about success.

## The Rise of "Aptitude" Testing

The idea that colleges should choose among applicants on the basis of their "academic ability" appeals to both educators and the public. But "ability" has two distinct meanings, which imply different admissions policies. In one usage, academic ability means an *existing* capacity to do academic work. In the other usage, academic ability means a *potential* capacity to do such work. To say that an applicant "has the ability to do differential calculus," for example, can mean either that the applicant can already do differential calculus or that the applicant could learn differential calculus given opportuity and motivation. To avoid this ambiguity psychometricians usually call the ability to learn something an "aptitude" while calling current mastery of a skill or body of knowledge "achievement."

When colleges say they want to select the "ablest" applicants, they almost always mean the applicants with the greatest academic "aptitude," not those with the highest current levels of academic "achievement." Yet so far as we know the United States is the only major industrial nation in which colleges and universities use so-called aptitude tests to help them make admissions decisions. This does not mean that British, French, German, Japanese, or Soviet universities are indifferent to aptitude as we have defined it. On the contrary, educators in these countries appear to be just as interested in their students' ability to learn as educators in the United States. Nonetheless, universities in other countries rely on what psychometricians call "achievement" tests rather than what they call "aptitude" tests to help them make admissions decisions. They do this because they assume that the best single predictor of how much a student will learn from studying something in a university is how much he or she learned from studying something similar in secondary school.

American colleges and universities made the same assumption until well into the twentieth century. In the nineteenth century most American colleges were so eager to get more students that they admitted virtually anyone who applied. Only a handful of elite institutions— mostly private colleges in the Northeast—tried to screen out unpromising students. They did this primarily by relying on grades and letters from secondary schools with which they had an on-going relationship. Most of these secondary schools were also private, but some were academically oriented public schools—again mostly in the Northeast. A number of selective private colleges also gave their own admission test, largely to determine whether students who did not come recommended by established secondary schools could do college-level work.

With the growth of public secondary education in the late nineteenth century students from far more secondary schools began applying to selective colleges, and the burden on colleges of administering their own admission test multiplied. In 1900 a number of selective private colleges established the College Entrance Examination Board to give a single set of admission tests to applicants all over the country.

Like the exams they replaced, the new College Board exams measured mastery of the subjects that academically oriented secondary schools had traditionally taught: ancient and modern languages, history, mathematics, and science. But many of the new public high schools did not teach these subjects or offered less than four years of instruction in them. For applicants from such schools, poor performance on the College Board exams did not necessarily imply poor performance in college. Such students would, it is true, usually have trouble in their first year, since they would not know a lot of things their professors assumed they knew. But if they survived their first year or two, such students often did better than their College Board scores might have led the college to expect. What the colleges therefore wanted was a test that would identify the "diamonds in the rough" who could be expected to overcome poor preparation and learn a lot if admitted. What they needed, in other words, was a measure of academic "aptitude."

American colleges were not, of course, the only institutions that wanted to measure aptitude. Elementary and secondary schools also wanted such a measure. Alfred Binet developed his original "intelligence" test to fill this need in France, and American variants of his test came into widespread use at the elementary and secondary level during the 1920s. The College Board administered its first Scholastic Aptitude Test in 1926. While the Board described the new test as a measure of "aptitude" rather than "intelligence," most people used the two terms almost interchangably at the time, and this is still true today. Both "aptitude" and "intelligence" were supposed to be stable traits that influenced behavior throughout life. In principle, of course, individuals' "aptitude" for higher education could depend on the quality of their secondary education. Then as now, however, most people used the term as if it referred to a stable trait. By calling the SAT an "aptitude" test, therefore, its designers were encouraging users to assume that it was insensitive to the quality of an individual's previous schooling.[1] They were also implicitly claiming that the SAT would predict college success more accurately than existing achievement tests. Had they not believed this, of course, they would not have developed or marketed the test in the first place.

To make the SAT insensitive to high school quality, its designers eschewed questions that obviously required skills or information taught only in "good" schools. Instead, they tried to measure skills and information that were taught either in all schools or in none. Virtually all elementary schools taught reading and arithmetic, for example, so the SAT included questions that tried to measure reading comprehension and arithmetic reasoning. Almost all secondary schools taught elementary algebra, so this too seemed a "fair" test of academic aptitude. And while good secondary schools tended to assign books that employed a larger vocabulary than the books assigned in mediocre schools, students from mediocre schools often acquired a large vocabulary from parents, friends, and extracurricular reading. The SAT therefore placed considerable emphasis on vocabulary and verbal fluency.

As time went on, colleges placed more emphasis on the SAT and less on the College Board's traditional achievement tests. Eventually, many colleges stopped requiring applicants to take the achievement tests at all. And when colleges that had previously relied entirely on high school grades for screening applicants began requiring applicants to take standardized tests as well, as many did in the 1960s and 1970s, they almost all required a test like the SAT, not achievement tests. The College Board does still offer one-hour multiple choice achievement tests in fourteen subjects, but only a fifth of those who take the SAT take even one achievement test.

ETS and the College Board have played a critical role in the shift from "achievement" to so-called aptitude tests. College admissions officers seldom have either the resources or the technical skills to make independent judgment about the merits of different kinds of tests. They rely on ETS and the College Board to do this for them. They emphasize the SAT because it purports to measure "aptitude," which is what they want to measure. They believe—wrongly as it turns out—that the SAT predicts future academic success more accurately than achievement tests can, and they think—again wrongly, as far as we can tell—that the quality of an applicant's secondary school preparation has less effect on SAT scores than on traditional achievement scores.

Until the 1960s ETS also seems to have believed the SAT measured a stable underlying trait of the kind that the label "aptitude" implied. In 1959, for example, ETS published a booklet by Martin Katz titled *You: Today and Tomorrow*, which was supposed to help ten-year-olds interpret their aptitude test scores. "In making their decisions," this booklet suggested, "the first questions that John, Andy, Betsy, and Bill have to ask themselves are these: How much general scholastic ability have I? What special abilities have I?" (Katz, 1959, p. 14). Later, it explained that "Your scholastic ability is like an engine. It is the source of your power and speed in school: It tells you how fast and how far you *can* go" (1959, p. 30).[2]

Since ETS gave tests that purported to measure scholastic ability, it seems reasonable to suppose that ETS thought scores on these tests were, in fact, like horsepower ratings on an engine.

ETS does not make such claims today. A great deal of evidence has now accumulated indicating that scores on tests like the SAT are not in fact stable. Not only do scores change over time but these changes also grow larger as the interval between tests lengthens, suggesting that the trends are real. More important for present purposes, scores on "aptitude" tests are no more stable than scores on conventional "achievement" tests. (See, for example, Shaycoft, 1967, or the correlations used by Alexander, Cook, and McDill, 1978.) The idea that "aptitude" tests measure stable traits better than "achievement" tests is therefore in disrepute among psychologists. Nonetheless, ETS and the College Board continue to call the SAT an "aptitude" test, which most people take to mean that it measures what they have always thought of as "aptitude," namely a stable trait.

### The Case for Relabeling the SAT

Jackson (1980, p. 383) formulates ETS's rationale for calling the SAT an "aptitude" test as follows. The SAT, he says, "measures intellectual skills learned through both formal and informal educational experiences—skills that are exercised and further developed through application to school work in a wide variety of academic subjects and through experiences outside of school." Note that this formulation implies that school quality is likely to affect SAT scores. Nonetheless, Jackson offers two rationales for calling the SAT an "aptitude" test. First, "it is not tied to a particular course of study." Second, "it is designed to assist in predicting future academic performance."[3]

Jackson's claim that SAT scores do not depend on "a particular course of study" is hard to reconcile with his assertion that they depend on "educational experiences" unless the relevant educational experiences do not vary from one course of study to another. This seems unlikely. Knowing the meaning of particular vocabulary words, for example, depends largely on having seen these words in context and having either inferred or investigated their meaning. A course of study that involves reading books written for adults is therefore likely to result in higher SAT scores than a course of study that relies on textbooks purged of unfamiliar terms. As we shall see, there is as much school-to-school variation in vocabulary, reading comprehension, and arithmetic reasoning scores as in scores on conventional secondary school achievement tests.

Jackson's argument that the SAT is an "aptitude" test because colleges use it to predict future academic performance is even less persuasive. Colleges use the results of all the tests they give applicants for either admission or placement decision. In either case, the tests are supposed to predict future performance. If this makes the SAT an "aptitude" test, it makes achievement tests in French and physics "aptitude" tests too. In one sense, of course, all these tests do measure aptitude. But if this is the only sense in which the SAT measures aptitude, the label is surely misleading.

If one defines aptitude as the capacity to master something, given opportunity and incentives, and achievement as having already mastered it, then almost every achievement test is also an aptitude test and almost every aptitude test is also an achievement test. If everyone taking an "achievement" test has had equal opportunities and incentives to master the material the test covers, those who interpret the test can assume that it measures "aptitude" as well as "achievement." But we cannot even approximate these conditions outside laboratory settings. College applicants have never had either equal opportunities or equal incentives to master anything. A "pure" measure of aptitude for higher education is therefore unattainable.

So why do ETS and other testing organizations persist in claiming certain tests measure "aptitude"? Why not just say the SAT measures vocabulary, reading comprehension, and quantitative reasoning? One possible answer is economic. Colleges *want* a measure of academic "aptitude" as distinct from "achievement." ETS is not in business to make money, but it must still worry about supporting its staff. If ETS were to give a vocabulary test, a reading comprehension test, and a basic mathematics test, scores on these tests would probably seem less significant to some college admissions offices, and some colleges might stop requiring applicants to take the test. Yet it is hard to believe this would happen on a large scale.

The main reason the SAT's label remains unchanged, despite all the changes in psychometric opinion about "aptitude" over the past generation, is probably institutional inertia. Why change the name of a product that is in such demand? Yet continuing to call the SAT a measure of "aptitude" involves significant risks. ETS is under increasing criticism from a variety of groups. Some of this criticism is mindless, but its pervasiveness means that ETS and other test designers must be extremely careful about maintaining their credibility among expert observers and test users. Claiming more for one's products than they can accomplish is a sure recipe for losing credibility and inviting legal restrictions on their use. The issue is not what ETS writes about the SAT in technical manuals or what ETS employees say about the SAT in academic journals. A test's name has more influence on how both educators and students interpret the results than technical manuals and scholarly articles can ever have. So long as ETS and the College Board call the SAT an "aptitude" test, people will assume it tries to measure "aptitude" in the traditional sense and will be understandably angry if they find that it does not in fact do this.

### The SAT Versus Other Achievement Tests: Predictive Validity

Reporting SAT scores as vocabulary, reading comprehension, and basic mathematics scores would not, of course, tell colleges whether to base their admission policies on these scores or on mastery of history, literature, physics, biology, and other secondary school subjects. In making this decision most colleges are likely to ask themselves two questions: which tests best predict college success, and which tests minimize the tendency of all admissions systems to favor white, middle-class applicants from elite schools? This section discusses the predictive powers of various tests.

*Freshman Grades.* So far as we know, the College Board did not investigate whether the SAT predicted college grades more or less accurately than traditional achievement tests when it first introduced the SAT in the 1920s. Since then there have been a number of studies in specific colleges, but results differ from college to college, and so far as we can discover there has been no study covering a large representative sample of college applicants. The best data we have found are from a study ETS conducted in 1979 of twenty-two highly selective colleges and universities. Seventy-eight percent of the freshmen in these colleges had taken at least one achievement test. Table 1 summarizes our analyses of these data. It shows that in the typical highly selective college SAT and achievement scores predict freshman grades equally well. In most colleges, scores on ETS's achievement tests are almost interchangeable with SAT scores. This suggests that colleges should choose between the two sorts of tests on grounds other than their ability to predict freshman grades.[4] Colleges committed to predicting applicants' grades as accurately as possible, regardless of the cost to the applicants, should obviously require both sorts of tests.

*College Completion.* So far as we know, ETS has not investigated whether its traditional achievement tests predict college completion better or worse than the SAT does, but one can get some relevant evidence from Project Talent. Talent surveyed a representative national sample of students who were in grades 9 through 12 of a public or private secondary school in 1960 and followed them up eleven years after their expected high school graduation, when they were around twenty-nine years old. We analyzed data on a representative subsample of those who had attended college.[5] To estimate college applicants' "aptitude" scores, we summed their scores on the Talent tests of vocabulary, reading comprehension, and arithmetic reasoning.[6] To estimate their overall "achievement" scores, we summed their standardized scores on the Talent

## Table 1. Mean $R^2$ in Regressions of Freshman Grade Point Average on Selected Student Characteristics in 22 Colleges

| Independent Variables | $R^2$ |
|---|---|
| 1. $SAT_V + SAT_M$ | .134 |
| 2. Achievement Scores | .134 |
| 3. High School Grades | .150 |
| 4. $SAT_V + SAT_M$ + High School Grades | .215 |
| 5. Achievement Scores + High School Grades | .213 |
| 6. $SAT_V + SAT_M$ + High School Grades + Achievement | .227 |
| 7. $SAT_V + SAT_M$ + Achievement | .151 |

Note: Achievement tests differ from college to college, and high school grades are based on grade-point average in some colleges and rank in class in others. Regressions for each college are available from Crouse on request. We are indebted to Len Ramist of ETS for supplying us with the original data.

tests covering English, history and social studies, mathematics, and natural sciences.[7]

Table 2 shows the correlations of the Talent "aptitude" and "achievement" composites, the number of years of higher education college entrants completed, and whether they earned a bachelor's degree. Among respondents initially tested in grade 12 who entered college, the standardized regression of the bachelor's degree (B.A.) variable on the "aptitude" and "achievement" composites is:

$$B.A. = 0.376 \text{ Achievement} + 0.026 \text{ Aptitude} \quad (R^2 = 0.158)$$

Since both coefficients have standard errors of 0.044, the "achievement" coefficient is highly significant while the "aptitude" coefficient is not at all significant.[8] This pattern recurs for respondents tested in ninth, tenth, and eleventh grades. It also recurs when one predicts years of higher education rather than earning a bachelor's degree, and when one adds high school grades to the equation.[9]

These results suggest that, at least in the 1960s, selective colleges could probably have reduced their attrition rates slightly if they had substituted a battery of achievement tests for the SAT. The reduction would not have been great, however, since the Talent aptitude and achievement composites correlate 0.82 among twelfth graders who attended college.

***Economic Success.*** Although colleges usually claim that their admissions policies are designed primarily to identify applicants who will do good academic work, many are also concerned with selecting applicants who will eventually be able to support the college financially. This concern is especially strong among highly selective private colleges, where alumni contributions play a major economic role. So far as we

**Table 2. Statistics on College Entrants in Project Talent**

| | Mean | S D | Aptitude | Achievement | High School Grades | Years of Higher Ed. | B.A. Degree |
|---|---|---|---|---|---|---|---|
| | | | | | Correlations | | |
| *Aptitude* | | | | | | | |
| 9th–12th | 106.48 | 13.20 | 1.000 | | | | |
| 12th only | 111.53 | 11.56 | 1.000 | | | | |
| *Achievement* | | | | | | | |
| 9th–12th | 105.98 | 11.16 | .859 | 1.000 | | | |
| 12th only | 110.58 | 10.91 | .824 | 1.000 | | | |
| *High School Grades* | | | | | | | |
| 9th–12th | 51.62 | 7.64 | .318 | .340 | 1.000 | | |
| 12th only | 51.21 | 7.40 | .362 | .379 | 1.000 | | |
| *Years of Higher Ed.* | | | | | | | |
| 9th–12th | 3.39 | 1.78 | .355 | .414 | .327 | 1.000 | |
| 12th only | 3.46 | 1.78 | .361 | .426 | .325 | 1.000 | |
| *B.A. Degree* | | | | | | | |
| 9th–12th | .52 | .50 | .356 | .396 | .331 | .816 | 1.000 |
| 12th only | .55 | .50 | .336 | .398 | .324 | .818 | 1.000 |

*Note:* Top rows cover 5,333 respondents who were initially surveyed in grades 9 through 12, attended college, and had complete data. Bottom rows cover 1,365 respondents initially surveyed in grade 12 who attended college and had complete data.

know, ETS has not examined the relationship of its achievement tests to adult economic success. Jencks, Crouse, and Mueser (1982) show, however, that the Talent "aptitude" and "achievement" composites we have just described are equally good predictors of adult economic success. If this were true for ETS tests as well, colleges could substitute conventional achievement tests for the SAT without any loss of information about applicants' future economic prospects.

## The SAT Versus Other Achievement Tests:
## Effects on Equal Opportunity

Although the SAT was originally supposed to help colleges identify able students from mediocre secondary schools, we have not been able to discover any research on whether it does this more effectively than achievement tests do. If the SAT were less sensitive than traditional achievement tests to variations in secondary school quality, schools' mean SAT scores should vary less relative to individual scores than schools' mean achievement scores do. Indeed, if the SAT were truly insensitive to the quality of the schools an individual had attended, schools' mean SAT scores should not vary at all once we controlled the characteristics of entering students.

Although ETS has not investigated the sensitivity of the SAT to school quality, it has conducted research that bears on the issue. The 1965 Equality of Educational Opportunity Survey (EEOS) administered tests of verbal ability, nonverbal ability, reading comprehension, and math achievement to about 100,000 twelfth graders in more than 800 public high schools. ETS designed the EEOS tests of verbal ability and reading comprehension, and many of the items were similar to those in the verbal section of the SAT. ETS also designed the math achievement test, using items from the mathematical achievement tests in its Sequential Tests of Educational Progress (STEP) series. Since the EEOS did not collect data on changes in individuals' test performance between ninth and twelfth grades, it does not provide direct evidence regarding the relative impact of high school quality on these tests. It does, however, provide some indirect evidence. Coleman and others (1966) report that schools' mean math achievement scores varied less relative to individual scores than schools' mean verbal ability or mean reading comprehension scores. This suggests, though it certainly does not suffice to prove, that variations in the quality of public high schools have less impact on math achievement than on verbal ability and reading comprehension.

We can get somewhat more satisfactory evidence regarding the relative impact of school quality on different sorts of tests from the longitudinal testing program carried out by Project Talent. In 1963 Talent retested about 7,000 twelfth graders whom it had initially tested as ninth graders in 1960. After controlling ninth-grade test scores, family background, and college plans, Jencks and Brown (1975) found that students who had said they were in a college preparatory curriculum in 1960 ended up with higher scores on Talent's twelfth-grade test of social studies and history information than otherwise comparable students who had said they were in a noncollege curriculum. The difference was about 0.11 standard deviations. Jencks and Brown made similar comparisons using Talent's tests of vocabulary, reading comprehension, arithmetic reasoning, and abstract reasoning—all of which contain questions similar to the SAT. On these four tests, twelfth graders who had been in the college preparatory curriculum averaged only 0.03 standard deviations above initially similar students who had been in some other curriculum. These results support Jackson's claim that so-called aptitude tests are less "tied to a particular course of study" than achievement tests are.

The fact that being in a college preparatory curriculum has less effect on "aptitude" than on "achievement" scores is not of much practical importance, however, since virtually all applicants to selective colleges have been in a college preparatory curriculum. From the colleges' viewpoint, the important question is whether school-to-school differences in the quality of college preparatory programs have more effect on "achievement" tests than on "aptitude" tests. Jencks and Brown (1975) found that after controlling the characteristics of entering ninth graders, variation in schools' mean achievement accounted for between 1.0 and 3.4 percent of the total variance in individual twelfth graders' vocabulary, reading comprehension, arithmetic reasoning, and abstract reasoning scores. The analogous figure for social studies and history information was 2.9 percent. This does not suggest that conventional achievement tests are any more sensitive to variations in high school quality than so-called aptitude tests are.

Both Coleman's findings and Jencks and Brown's raise serious doubts about the College Board's traditional assumption that the SAT places applicants from secondary schools of varying quality on a more equal footing than achievement tests do. This assumption may have been correct half a century ago, when the SAT was instituted, and it may still be correct today if one compares the SAT to achievement tests in subjects that are only taught in a limited number of secondary schools. But so far as we can tell from the limited available evidence, it is not likely to be true for achievement tests in subjects like mathematics and social studies that are taught, albeit in very diverse ways, in all secondary schools.

*Inequality Between Families.* So far as we can discover, ETS has not investigated whether race and socioeconomic status (SES) affect conventional achievement scores as strongly as they affect SAT scores. Heyns's (1978) work on summer learning suggests that both race and SES have more impact on what students learn outside the classroom than inside it. Thus, if the SAT were less tied to classroom learning than conventional achievement tests are, we would expect race and SES to have more impact on SAT scores than on conventional achievement scores. But as we have seen, the SAT may in fact be just as tied to classroom learning as conventional achievement tests are. Here as elsewhere, we need evidence to choose between the plethora of potentially plausible theories.

ETS's Academic Growth Study (AGS) surveyed ninth graders in 1965 and followed them up in eleventh and twelfth grades. The AGS gave ninth graders both "aptitude" and "achievement" tests, gave eleventh graders a battery of achievement tests, and gave twelfth graders either the SAT or PSAT. Unpublished correlations from Alexander, Cook, and McDill (1978) indicate that the AGS's "aptitude" and "achievement" scores correlate 0.87 in ninth grade and 0.84 in eleventh and twelfth grades. Father's education, father's occupation, and mother's education have mean correlations of 0.234 with the two "aptitude" scores and of 0.236 with the two "achievement" scores. The mean correlations for race are 0.255 versus 0.267. These figures suggest that for those concerned with equality of opportunity the choice between so-called aptitude tests and conventional achievement tests is a toss-up.

**The SAT Versus Other Achievement Tests:**
**Effects on High Schools**

The evidence we have just reviewed indicates that tests like the SAT do not measure what we normally mean by "aptitude" any better than conventional achievement tests do. SAT scores appear to be just as dependent on home environment and school quality as scores on conventional achievement tests. And conventional achievement tests predict success in college and adult life just as well as the SAT or other "aptitude" tests do. Many at ETS conclude from this that while the SAT is no better than conventional achievement tests, it is no worse, either. We disagree. The reason we disagree is that we think emphasizing tests like the SAT in college admissions undermines efforts to improve secondary education.

Both college teachers and the general public have become increasingly concerned in recent years with the fact that freshmen know less than they used to. The decline in mean SAT scores is the most publicized symptom of this problem, but other testing programs have found the same trend. The problem is not that primary school children aren't mastering the three R's as well as they used to. If anything, they are doing better. But teenagers are not moving as far beyond the three R's as they used to (Jencks, 1981).

Talking to high school students, teachers, and parents, one gets the strong impression that high school students do less academic work today than they did twenty years ago. Yet their nominal grades are higher than they were twenty years ago. This means that a clever student can earn A's without learning much. Such students know that if they earn A's in high school and do well on the SAT they will be able to get into a top college. And they assume—erroneously in many cases—that because they got A's without doing much work, they must be "smart" and therefore likely to do well on the SAT. If they then do badly, they often blame the test rather than their school.

Although we have no quantitative data on the number of hours secondary school students in different countries spend studying, most observers agree that American high school students do less academic work than their counterparts in Europe or Japan. Most observers also agree that one crucial reason—perhaps *the* crucial reason—European and Japanese teenagers work hard is that they must take achievement tests at the end of secondary school that largely determine whether and where they will be allowed to obtain higher education. We would not want to see American teenagers become as preoccupied with academic success and exams as, say, Japanese teenagers are, but this is not a real danger. We *would* like to see American teenagers do more academic work than they now do. If selective colleges were to base admission on high school grades and tests that measured mastery of the secondary school curriculum instead of basing it on grades and tests that measure vocabulary, reading comprehension, and basic mathematics, high school students who wanted to attend selective colleges might take their academic work somewhat more seriously.

Emphasizing mastery of the secondary school curriculum would have other benefits as well. First, it would help reinforce the traditional American notion that effort will be rewarded. Emphasizing the SAT, in contrast, reinforces the notion that working harder won't help much and that success depends on factors like "smarts" over which you have no control. As we have seen, this notion is probably mistaken, since the SAT is also an achievement test. But neither students nor teachers fully realize this. If we want high school students to believe work pays off, colleges must not only reward applicants who have worked hard but also do so in an obvious way.

Emphasizing tests that measure mastery of secondary school subjects would also encourage such schools to offer more demanding academic courses. One should not, of course, exaggerate the potential impact of college admission tests on high school curricula. Only about half the nation's high school graduates attend college, and only a handful even apply to selective colleges where test scores play a major role in admission decisions.[10] This minority does, however, influence the overall character of secondary education in a way disproportionate to its numbers. Those who attend selective colleges often come from influential families, and many educators judge their school's overall success by such students' accomplishments. Furthermore, while such students are not always social leaders in their schools, they typically exert more overall influence on their peers than their peers exert on them. Changes in college admissions policy that affect these students therefore tend to have ripple effects on secondary schools as a whole.

The effect of substituting conventional achievement tests for the SAT would depend, of course, on how the new systems worked. If all colleges were to require conventional achievement tests, more secondary schools would feel obliged to offer courses explicitly tailored to such tests. Those who oppose such exams usually point with horror to their consequences in France; those who favor them usually point to England, where national exams have produced more curricular uniformity than in America but far less than in France. Given the small proportion of American students applying to selective colleges, national exams would probably have even less impact here than in England. Furthermore, if our concern is with maintaining diversity, it would be easy to establish a set of achievement tests more flexible than those used in either France or England.

The College Board now offers achievement tests in fourteen subjects. If more colleges were concerned with measuring achievement, ETS could easily double or triple this number, even giving several types of exams in the most popular subjects. If the College Board allowed students to take as many exams as they wanted, while only reporting their highest scores, students could take a lot of unorthodox courses without jeopardizing their admissions prospects. Such a system would still reward "smarts," as the SAT does, but it would also require and reward sustained application in at least a few areas, which the present system does not.

## Conclusion

Since the argument up to this point has been somewhat convoluted, it may help if we recapitulate. Most discussions of college admissions policy focus on distributive justice. They ask whether the existing system admits the students somebody thinks selective colleges "ought" to admit. If we apply criteria of this kind, the choice between the SAT and conventional achievement tests appears, on present evidence, to be a tossup. Both are equally helpful in identifying applicants who will earn above-average grades, who will finish college rather than drop out, and who will be more successful than average after they graduate. Both pose comparable obstacles to blacks, working-class whites, and applicants from second-rate high schools.

But we must also ask how college admissions policies affect the behavior of secondary school students, teachers, and administrators. Because this issue is harder to quantify, experts tend to ignore it. But in the long run it may be even more important than the questions of distributive justice about which experts mostly worry. A good college admissions system should encourage diligence rather than sloth and seriousness rather than frivolity among secondary school students. The present system does not seem to us to do this. Selective colleges today base their admissions decisions largely on grades and SAT scores. Some high schools distribute grades in such a way as to promote diligence and seriousness, but many do not. Because of both its content and its name, the SAT does not appear to reward diligence. Furthermore, by emphasizing skills that secondary schools do not explicitly teach, at least after tenth grade, the SAT implicitly tells secondary schools that most of what they do teach does not really matter. It is always hard to defend a curriculum concerned with what Matthew Arnold called "the best that has been thought and said." Lacking external support, American secondary schools have largely stopped trying. The time has come for colleges to give them some help.

## Notes

1. For critical assessments of the ideas about testing held by the creators of mental testing, the founders of ETS, and the designers of the SAT, see Kamin (1974) and Nairn and Associates (1980).

2. See Nairn and Associates (1980) and Slack and Porter (1980a, 1980b) for additional evidence that until very recently ETS has described the SAT as a measure of academic potential, although as Jackson (1980) says, such claims have usually been hedged by noting that aptitude tests are not perfectly reliable and that scores occasionally change over time. (See, for example, Katz, 1959, pp. 20–21.)

3. Messick and Jungeblut (1981) formulate ETS's position in similar terms.

4. Because these colleges did not admit many students with low SAT scores, SAT scores do not explain as much of the variation in freshman grades at these colleges as they do at less selective colleges. The admissions process probably restricts the range of SAT scores more than the range of achievement scores, although the high correlation between SAT and achievement scores means that the difference is not likely to be appreciable. On the other hand, selective test taking may restrict the range of achievement scores relative to SAT scores. Furthermore, the fact that some students took only one or two achievement tests may make achievement scores less reliable than SAT scores in this sample. Thus, achievement scores could predict freshman grades either slightly better or slightly worse than SAT scores if we had equally reliable scores on samples with equally restricted ranges.

5. About a quarter of the initial sample returned a mail follow-up. Talent drew 3 to 4 percent subsamples of nonrespondents each year and followed them up intensively, obtaining data from 80 to 85 percent of these individuals. Our sample includes 3 to 4 percent of the initial mail respondents and all those in the subsample that was followed up intensively. The effective response rate is thus about (0.25) + (0.75) (0.83) = 87 percent.

6. Because the reading comprehension test is longer than the other two and has a larger standard deviation, it dominates the aptitude composite. Jencks,

Crouse, and Mueser (1982) show, however, that this fact does not account for the aptitude composite's weak relationship to educational attainment.

7. Our "English" score includes not only knowledge of English literature but mastery of "proper" English, measured by tests of punctuation, capitalization, usage, and the like. Dropping the "proper" English component of the composite slightly increases its correlation with eventual educational attainment among eleventh graders. Jencks, Crouse, and Mueser (1981) give additional details on the construction of the composites and their correlations with other variables.

8. Since the aptitude composite correlates more highly than the achievement composite with race ($r = 0.29$ versus $0.25$), father's education ($r = 0.22$ versus $0.21$), father's occupational status ($r = 0.25$ versus $0.23$), and mother's education ($r = 0.20$ versus $0.19$), we assume the aptitude composite is at least as reliable as the achievement composite. Shaycoft's (1967) estimates of split-half reliabilities support this assumption.

9. Because Talent asked high school students to report their own grades since ninth grade and used ambiguous reporting categories, Table 2 underestimates the correlation of high school grades with other variables.

10. Based on a sample survey of 200 four-year colleges, Hartnett and Feldmesser (1980) estimate that a third of all four-year colleges admit more than 90 percent of their applicants, slightly over half admit more than 80 percent, four fifths admit more than 70 percent, and nine tenths admit more than 50 percent. We know of only six private colleges that admitted fewer than 25 percent of their applicants in 1979, namely Amherst (14 percent), Harvard-Radcliffe (18 percent), Princeton, Stanford, and Williams (23 percent each), and Yale (24 percent).

## References

Alexander, K. L., Cook, M., and McDill, E. L. "Curriculum Tracking and Educational Stratification." *American Sociological Review*, 1978, *43* (1), 47–66.

Coleman, J. S., and others. *Equality of Educational Opportunity.* Washington, D.C.: U.S. Government Printing Office, 1966.

Hartnett, R. F., and Feldmesser, R. A. "College Admissions Testing and the Myth of Selectivity." *AAHE Bulletin*, 1980, *32* (7), 3–6.

Heyns, B. L. *Summer Learning and the Effects of Schooling.* New York: Academic Press, 1978.

Jackson, R. "The Scholastic Aptitude Test: A Response to Slack and Porter's Critical Appraisal." *Harvard Educational Review*, 1980, *50* (3), 382–391.

Jencks, C. "Declining Test Scores: An Assessment of Six Alternative Explanations." *Sociological Spectrum*, 1981, *1* (1), 1–15.

Jencks, C., and Brown, M. "The Effects of High Schools on Their Students." *Harvard Educational Review*, 1975, *45*, 273–324.

Jencks, C., Crouse, J., and Mueser, P. "The Wisconsin Model of Status Attainment: A National Replication with Improved Measures of Ability and Aspirations." *Sociology of Education*, 1982, in press.

Kamin, L. J. *The Science and Politics of IQ.* Potomac, Md.: Erlbaum, 1974.

Katz, M. R. *You: Today and Tomorrow.* Princeton, N.J.: Cooperative Test Division, Educational Testing Service, 1959.

Messick, S., and Jungeblut, A. "Time and Method in Coaching for the SAT." *Psychological Bulletin*, 1981, *89*, 191–216.

Nairn, A., and Associates. *The Reign of ETS: The Corporation that Makes Up Minds.* Washington, D.C.: Ralph Nader, 1980.

Shaycoft, M. *The High School Years: Growth in Cognitive Skills.* Pittsburgh: Project Talent, 1967.

Slack, W. V., and Porter, D. "The Scholastic Aptitude Test: A Critical Appraisal." *Harvard Educational Review*, 1980a, *50* (2), 154–175.

Slack, W. V., and Porter, D. "Training, Validity, and the Issue of Validity: A Reply to Jackson." *Harvard Educational Review*, 1980b, *50* (3), 392–401.

*Christopher Jencks is professor of sociology and urban affairs, Northwestern University.*

*James Crouse is professor of educational studies, University of Delaware.*

*The three commenters express mixed reactions to the
proposals offered by Jencks and Crouse.*

# Comments on "Should We Relabel the SAT . . . or Replace It?"

Ronald R. Edmonds
John D. Krumboltz
William A. Mehrens

## Comments: Ronald R. Edmonds

My first response is to endorse the present uses of the SAT while strongly
sharing Jencks and Crouse's questioning of the label of the SAT. In recent
years, the American discourse on educational equity has been considerably advanced by discussions of school effectiveness. We are increasingly
certain that pupil acquisition of school skills is primarily a function of
school characteristics. That is a considerable advance over our historic
preoccupation with familial effects as chief explanation for pupil
performance.

Jencks and Crouse are correct in focusing attention on "aptitude"
as the pupil trait presumably measured by the SAT. If, as Jencks and
Crouse persuasively argue, the SAT is in fact an achievement test, then it
helps neither schools nor students to label the principal instrument of
college admission as measuring a trait about which neither schools nor
students can do very much.

W. Schrader (Ed.). *New Directions for Testing and Measurement: Measurement,
Guidance, and Program Improvement,* no. 13. San Francisco: Jossey-Bass, March 1982.    51

The mislabeling of the SAT is doubly unfortunate. First, it emphasizes things that presumably the school can't teach, which is needlessly discouraging. Second, the SAT is a reasonably good achievement test for the purpose for which it is used; relabeled there would be little reason to be as profoundly critical as are Jencks and Crouse. I therefore hope to see an early and thoughtful response to this work by Jencks and Crouse, resulting in a more accurate description of the SAT. Accuracy is, after all, one of the measures of good testing.

## The Unintended Social Consequences of Testing: John D. Krumboltz

Jencks and Crouse have forcefully reminded us that our testing policies have consequences that reach far beyond those benevolently intended by the test makers and test users. Certain assumptions involved in the use of these tests may be unintentionally communicated and uncritically accepted by those directly affected.

Perhaps the essential question is this: What do we want our young people to believe: (1) that success in life is the result of studious effort and hard work or (2) that success is the result of being born with "smarts" or being surrounded by a bubble of affluence? Jencks and Crouse imply that a possible danger of the current SAT is that it may be unwittingly fostering the belief that success in life is pretty much predetermined by one's genetic endowment and perhaps by the socioeconomic class into which one has been born. If the SAT is seen as a test that measures one's inherent abilities, then there is no use studying for it because success or failure will occur regardless of one's efforts.

What difference would it make if the SAT were labeled the Scholastic Achievement Test instead of the Scholastic Aptitude Test? Probably a cosmetic name change by itself would not have much impact. There can be no doubt, however, that the SAT, by whatever title it is called, is in fact an achievement test. I don't think anyone would deny that the SAT measures what people have learned in the past.

Whether a test is labeled as an aptitude or achievement test usually depends upon its intended use. Aptitude tests are presumably used to predict future performance. Achievement tests are used to assess prior performance. But even interest tests can be thought of as achievement tests since one's self-reported interest is often a function of successful or unsuccessful past attempts at achievement. Indeed, one interest test, the Michigan Vocabulary Profile, was developed in 1939 on the premise that one's knowledge of specialized vocabulary was evidence of preferences.

There is no question but that so-called achievement tests predict future performance just as well as so-called aptitude tests. The regression equation presented by Jencks and Crouse, based on the data in their

Table 2, is misleading in suggesting that achievement is a far better predictor than aptitude. Their simulated aptitude test consisted of only three subtests while their simulated achievement test consisted of four. A longer test tends to be more reliable and hence tends to correlate higher with any criterion. Furthermore, comparing the size of beta weights in a regression equation is highly misleading, since the predictor entered first carries the common variance. If the order of variables entered into the equation had been reversed, the aptitude test would have had the higher beta weight. However, Jencks and Crouse acknowledge that the difference between the two is insignificant inasmuch as the two composites correlate .82 with each other.

Suppose we were to make it a matter of educational policy to encourage the notion in young people that the road to success in our society is achieved through effort and hard work. We would then devise our tests to show in every respect possible that hard work paid off. We would not discourage people from being "coached" on tests. On the contrary, the coaching would be encouraged in scholastic endeavors as much as in athletics. We would help teachers see how their subject matters related to the abilities measured by the SAT. We would help them see that mere memorization alone was insufficient to do well, that critical thinking ability needed to be taught. Members of minority groups would not be discouraged from attempting to perform well because of factors over which they had no control; on the contrary, they would be given educational experiences that would help them perform well.

The notion that testing policies might influence student behavior is an exciting idea, but it should come as no surprise. Students have known this for years. In the opening day of any class session, the teacher usually outlines the objectives of the course. The students wait patiently for the lecture to finish so that they can ask the inevitable questions: What do we have to do to pass? Is there going to be a final exam? Will it be essay, short answer, multiple choice, or true-false? What will the exam cover? Do we have to write a paper? Do you count off for spelling? The students want to know the rules that will enable them to survive. And they realize that there is often a difference between stipulated rules and the rules applied in practice. Their study behavior is a function of the rules they believe actually apply.

If this is true in individual classrooms, might it not be equally true for nationwide testing programs? To what extent are student beliefs and work habits affected by the nature of the SAT and the publicity about it? We don't know. We do know, on the basis of some studies, that the way in which students study for classroom tests depends upon the format of the tests, whether they are essay or multiple choice, for example. But do we know whether relabeling the SAT as an achievement test would produce any differences in student behavior and beliefs? More than labels, the whole rationale and set of presuppositions that underlie each form of the test would need to be compared. Certainly the issue lends itself to empirical study. If ETS is looking for a research question on which to employ their talented stable of educational researchers, the question of the effects of induced cognitive sets on study behavior and test performance would be a good place to start.

## Comments: William A. Mehrens

The chapter by Jencks and Crouse will certainly stir up interest and, I suspect, controversy among the ETS and College Board personnel who must ultimately decide whether to implement or ignore their suggestions. I would hate to be in their shoes. I am ambivalent. Further, ETS will be damned by someone whatever they decide to do. In this response, I shall discuss briefly the aptitude and achievement distinction and then conjecture on the likely impact of relabeling or replacing the SAT.

The distinctions and similarities between the concepts and measures of aptitude and achievement have been the subject of much debate. I submit that there would be general but not total agreement among psychometricians on the following points: (1) General aptitude tests typically have broader coverage than achievement tests. (2) Achievement tests are more closely tied to particular school subjects. (3) Achievement tests typically measure recent learning, whereas aptitude tests sample learning from all times in the individual's past. (4) Studies generally show that aptitude tests have higher heritability indexes than achievement tests. (5) The purpose of aptitude tests is to predict future performance; the purpose of achievement tests is to measure the present level of knowledge or skills. (6) Both aptitude and achievement test scores are subject to change.

Anastasi, Ebel, and Snow all discussed the aptitude-achievement issue at the 1979 ETS Invitational Conference. Snow suggested that the SAT "is a test of *extended* or *generalized* achievement designed to be indicative of aptitude for college work, that is, for work requiring broader, deeper, higher, and more elaborate organizations and reorganizations of scholastic learning than that represented *directly* in prior public schooling" (Snow, 1980, pp. 43–44; italics in original). He goes on to say that one important goal of earlier education should be to develop this *aptitude* for later education.

Although Anastasi would banish both the words *aptitude* and *achievement*, she recognizes that the traditional distinction in the usage of the terms is in "the degree of precision with which relevant antecedent experience is defined" and "the way the test scores are utilized" (Anastasi, 1980, pp. 1, 7, and 8).

It seems to me that Jackson (1980) is in the mainstream of the psychometric community with his two rationales for calling the SAT an "aptitude" test—that is, it is not tied to a particular course of study, and it is designed to assist in predicting future academic performance. From a psychometric point of view, I do not believe accuracy of labeling is at issue. The test is an aptitude test in the traditional psychometric sense of the word.

What about the accuracy of the public's perception? Does the public subscribe to all those incorrect beliefs ascribed to them? I believe not. I just do not believe the often heard argument that people infer complete stability from the term *aptitude*. I have never heard of anyone who would admit to believing that aptitude scores were not susceptible to change. The critics of our public schools that Jencks and Crouse refer to, who argue (incorrectly in my opinion) that the SAT score decline is symptomatic of the decline of our public schools, certainly do not believe the scores are unaffected by education. Thus I really do not foresee any impact of a name change on high school students' study habits or high school curriculum makers.

I wish, however, to go on record as agreeing with the point Jencks and Crouse have made regarding student study habits. I would also like to see American high school students work harder in school. But those students who are already striving for admission to selective colleges are not the ones who need additional motivation to study. They, by and large, already have a need to achieve, or they would not want to attend a college with high academic admissions standards. Changing the name of the SAT or changing the test would not have much effect on these students. The ones who do not plan to attend selective colleges obviously do not care what the test is called or what kind of test it is.

I believe that the ACT tests and the new Medical College Admissions Test (MCAT) are nearer the achievement end of the aptitude and achievement continuum than the SAT or the old MCAT. I know of no data suggesting that students taking the ACT study harder in high school than those taking the SAT or that students taking the new MCAT study more in college than students taking the old MCAT.

If we really wish to use college entrance examinations to affect high school students' study habits, we should change the *level* of admission standards. As long as we have major four-year colleges admitting students who need to take sixth-grade arithmetic in college, it will not help much to change the name or nature of the exam.

What about their contention that relabeling or replacing the SAT will affect the secondary school curriculum? Both I and the College Board agree with Jencks and Crouse that the secondary school curriculum should be improved. The goal of College Board's Project EQuality (College Entrance Examination Board, 1981) is to improve the academic preparation of college-bound students. Project EQuality has reached some consensus with a broad cross section of the educational community on what academic preparation for college ought to be. They have identified six learning skills on basic academic competencies (reading, writing, listening and speaking, doing mathematics, reasoning, and studying) and a basic academic curriculum covering six subjects (English, mathematics, history and social studies, foreign or second language, natural science, and visual and performing arts). (As you all know, the ACT tests purport to measure four of these six areas.) To my knowledge, the College Board wisely has not suggested that the role they wish to play in upgrading secondary schooling should use admissions tests as the catalyst. Would such an approach even work?

Relabeling the SAT probably would have little effect on the secondary school curriculum, but to replace the SAT with or add tests more closely tied to particular courses of study probably would have an effect. The question is, how big an effect and would it be for good or ill? The position of Jencks and Crouse seems to be that the effect would be great enough to be positive, but not so great that it would be negative. They may be correct. But we have heard before the charge that a major problem with public schools is that test publishers dictate curriculum. Now we have heard that a major problem with the public schools is that the SAT does not affect the curriculum. (Why can't those ETS people get their act together?)

I am reasonably sure that if admission to colleges were based more on published achievement tests tied more closely to identifiable courses of study, we would have even more of an outcry from the antitesters with respect to curricular encroachment. I am also reasonably sure it would result in even greater profits to coaching schools. I suspect that Jencks and Crouse's contention that such tests would encourage more demanding academic courses in high school is correct. That, of course, would not necessarily be beneficial to the students not bound for college.

Finally, I urge you all to read an article by Scarr and Yee (1980) in the *Educational Psychologist*. Based on their research, they concluded that "the more a test samples what has recently and explicitly been taught in school, the more differences in adolescents' social environments account for differences in performance" (Scarr and Yee, 1980, p. 1). Whether or not it would be more fair to base selective college admissions decisions on measures of specifically taught material rather than more global measures depends on one's definition of fairness. But such a change in strategy would not be likely to reduce the variance accounted for by socioeconomic status.

57

## References

Anastasi, A. "Abilities and the Measurement of Achievement." In W. B. Schrader (Ed.), *New Directions for Testing and Measurement: Measuring Achievement: Progress over a Decade,* no. 5. San Francisco: Jossey-Bass, 1980.
College Entrance Examination Board. *Project EQuality.* New York: College Entrance Examination Board, September 1981.
Ebel, R. L. "Achievement Tests as Measures of Developed Abilities." In W. B. Schrader (Ed.), *New Directions for Testing and Measurement: Measuring Achievement: Progress over a Decade,* no. 5. San Francisco: Jossey-Bass, 1980.
Jackson, R. "The Scholastic Aptitude Test: A Response to Slack and Porter's Critical Appraisal." *Harvard Educational Review,* 1980, *50* (3), 382–391.
Scarr, S., and Yee, D. "Heritability and Educational Policy: Genetic and Environmental Effects on IQ, Aptitude, and Achievement." *Educational Psychologist,* 1980, *15* (1), 1–22.
Snow, R. E. "Aptitude and Achievement." In W. B. Schrader (Ed.), *New Directions for Testing and Measurement: Measuring Achievement: Progress over a Decade,* no. 5. San Francisco: Jossey-Bass, 1980.

*Ronald R. Edmonds is professor of education, Michigan State University.*

*John D. Krumboltz is professor of education and psychology, Stanford University.*

*William A. Mehrens is professor of measurement and evaluation, Michigan State University.*

*Recent studies throw a great deal of light on*
*how tests are used and how they should be used*
*to improve education.*

# If "How to Improve Schools" Is the Question, Are Tests Part of the Answer?

*Lois-ellin Datta*

There is something of a paradox in efforts to tie tests to school improvement. At building and classroom levels, teacher-made tests, craft knowledge, and principal observations are the primary sources of insight data. Norm-referenced or criterion-referenced achievement test results are used only in a few situations, such as very sensitive pupil placement or grouping decisions made at the beginning of the school year. Greater use at classroom and building levels has been viewed as a key to school improvement. Most efforts intended to increase the utility of tests for school improvement thus are classroom focused, and indeed work in this direction seems methodologically most advanced.

Opinions expressed are the author's in her private capacity. Endorsement by the National Institute of Education should not be inferred. My thanks to reviewers Marvin Alkin, Mary Ann Millsap, Ann Drennan, Judith Shoemaker and Mary Kennedy.

Meanwhile at federal, state, and district levels, achievement tests provide the primary sources of "oversight" data about what is happening in schools and the educational state of the nation. They now are used mainly as prods. If the scores go up, we are encouraged to feel renewed confidence in education, to continue supporting programs taking the credit, to put more resources into whatever is the senior claimant for the fame. If scores go down, we flail around, often convening national commissions to consider the relative weight to be given to general permissiveness, divorce, television, teacher incompetence, outdated curricula, too much or too little in-school time, and misguided educational practices. Yet scant attention has been given to whether such use of test results leads to improvement.

The next sections of this chapter present information on the prevalence of testing and findings from recent studies on how tests are used at building and classroom levels for insights on better instruction, and at local, state, and national levels for oversight of educational progress.

## The Prevalence of Achievement-Related Testing

Achievement-related testing is now an accepted fact of life in public education at local, state, and national levels (Resnick, 1982).

### At the Local Level

1. Lyon and others (1978), in the first national survey of all school district evaluation offices, found their activities centered on student testing. About 75 percent of the evaluation directors indicated student achievement testing was their dominant activity.

2. Twenty-six of the twenty-nine members of the Council of Great City Schools (the nation's largest school systems) operated locally established minimum competency testing programs.

3. 90 percent of all local education agencies administer standardized norm-referenced tests.

4. In 1975–76, school systems collectively spent about $24 million annually on testing.

### In Response to State Requirements

1. Thirty-five mandated minimum competency testing programs and thirty states operate some type of statewide achievement assessment program (Gorth and Perkins, 1979).

### In Response to Federal Programs

1. According to Anderson (1982), "As many as 75 percent to 95 percent of all students in special programs such as bilingual or Title I are likely to be tested annually for evaluation purposes, often at both the beginning and end of the year" (p. 243).

2. The National Assessment of Educational Progress is administered annually to about 29,000 nine-year-olds; 41,000 thirteen-year-olds;
and 36,000 seventeen-year-olds.

Cumulatively, that's a lot of tests. Houts (1975) estimated that each
student in the United States receives six to twelve full batteries of tests
between kindergarten and the twelfth grade, which does not include special achievement tests, locally developed diagnostic tests, testing done
through the National Assessment of Educational Progress, state required
competency tests, or teacher-made classroom tests. Yeh (1980) reports that
two million achievement test forms are used yearly, "and this number
represents only about 65 percent of all educational and psychological
testing that is carried out" (p. 1).

Testing requirements are distributed unevenly across student
groups. Anderson (1982) found that achievement-related testing, exclusive
of teacher-made tests and special diagnostic tests, involves about six hours
annually for most students between third and twelfth grades. She reports,
however, that "students in compensatory or special education programs
may experience two or three times as much" (p. 251), that is, up to three
days a year of achievement testing.

Together, achievement-related tests required at local, state, and
federal levels represent a significant investment of student time, particularly for low-income and underachieving students, and of the time of
instructional and noninstructional personnel. With regard to student
time, Denham and Lieberman (1980), among others, have shown that
achievement is related directly to engaged learning time. At typical
engaged learning time rates (Rosenshine, 1980), reallocating the eighteen
hours of tests annually for an average, low-income fifth-grade student
would be the equivalent of adding almost a full month of schooling in
mathematics or two weeks of direct instruction in reading. Rudman et al.
(1980) note that while testing time often is challenged, there is no corres-
ponding skepticism about planning and instruction, although planning
also takes time away from the school day (p. 3). The Austin schools
(Holley and Ligon, 1980), however, regarded as a substantial improvement changes in the management of instructional time that yielded the
equivalent of one more day annually per student at no additional direct
cost.

## Little Building and Classroom Use Today

As part of their study of eighteen school districts using evaluation
and test data in exemplary ways, Kennedy, Apling and Neuman (1980)
surveyed teachers and found that, in most cases, teachers' professional
judgments "played a more significant role in instruction than tests did"
(p. 87). With regard to grouping children or placing them in special

programs, teachers seemed to "prefer using more than one criterion and more than one person to make the decision. They were uneasy about the consequences to the child of making a mistake and they sensed the falli- bility of the various assessment devices at their disposal" (p. 93). Observa- tion was the preferred source of knowledge, tests "being used to supplement that knowledge when it seemed too scanty—at the beginning of the year, when teachers had to group children they did not know very well, or when a teacher suspected a child should be referred to a special program" (p. 95).

The reliance of teachers on their professional knowledge, rather than on tests, is consistent with the results of the Kellaghan, Madaus, and Airasian's (1980) studies of the introduction of standardized testing in Ireland. They conclude: "Standardized test results do not have a great deal of salience in the teacher's information web. Test information in most cases serves to confirm the evaluations of pupils' ability and achievement which teachers have already formed. Thus it will be the exception rather than the rule for a teacher to be confronted with information from tests which might lead her or him to believe that some modification of her or his perceptions or practices should be considered. However, when there is a discrepancy, test results are often used to improve the teacher's percep- tions of the student's ability, rarely to lower it. . . . our findings provide no evidence to support the position that standardized testing when based in classrooms under the control of teachers differs in kind in its effects from any other evaluation procedure available to the teacher" (pp. 905– 908). The similarities are perhaps surprising in light of the many years experience with standardized achievement tests in the United States and the brevity of the teachers' experiences with them in Ireland. Those who see tests as the answer to some educational problems through reduced dependence on what is regarded as imperfect or biased teacher judgments in educational decisions affecting individual children can find little com- fort in the data. Teachers indicate continued reliance on their own obser- vations and craft knowledge in the classroom.

As heard by Kennedy, Apling and Neuman (1980), dominant con- cerns of building principals are district policies (for example, rules speci- fying when students can be pulled from classrooms for special programs, or procedures for disciplining students for absenteeism or fighting), building management (teacher and student morale, school atmosphere, racial tensions, student behavior and discipline, and instructional management), and program involvement (primarily curricular changes). As seen by these principals, most district-wide data systems available to them focus on student achievement (instructional management); there is little district-wide information on the issues of most con- cern to them—district policies and building management other than instruction.

Several principals *did* rely on test scores to improve instruction: "I look at the scores to see where I should be concerned. I look by school and by teacher to see which teachers have low scores. I have two conferences with each teacher (fall and spring), and we [review] each objective, and we go over how they did and how it compares to the school average. . . . they come up with their own group growth plan which should incorporate our discussion about their areas of weakness" (Kennedy, Apling, and Neuman, 1980, p. 71).

These principals were exceptions; most relied on observation rather than on systematic data to tell them what they want to know about building atmosphere and morale: ". . . Do the teachers volunteer for assembly detail? When I see a group of students gambling outside of school, do they stop when they see me coming? Are copies of the school newspaper thrown on the floor or are they read and taken home?" (1980, p. 73). The district-level monitoring systems are seen as being of no use for dealing with the real problems the principals face in managing the school and implementing district policies and of little use for instructional improvement: "The reading scores at the end of the year don't tell you anything. That kind of information does not tell you how to run a building or organize a school. Maybe the new [criterion referenced test] will help the teachers but it won't help the administrators" (p. 72–73). Curricular improvement was rarely discussed: Kennedy and her colleagues speculate that in addition to the impediments of lack of time and constraints imposed by district level procedures, "[curricular] improvement is rare because people aren't sure what they should strive for, and hence what they should be doing differently" (p. 80).

Test use today, or rather lack of it, at classroom and building levels seems to have changed little over the past twenty-five years. In their masterful review of research on the integration of assessment with instruction, Rudman and others (1980) observed that while earlier beliefs about teacher antipathy toward tests may be overgeneralizations, and teachers favor greater use than measurement specialists believe they do, actual use has not increased greatly over the modest levels reported for 1950–1954 by Goslin (1967). Rudman remarks: "Teachers have, for many years, been testing students with a variety of instruments . . . but testing for the most part has been summative . . . It has been used to rate pupil progress rather than to monitor it. There is little evidence to indicate that teachers use their own tailor-made tests analytically to identify modalities on which to build learning experiences. Testing, while not new to the educational process, has been separate from it" (1980, p. 4).

There could be some argument for letting well enough alone. Rudman and his colleagues, for example, could not find evidence on whether there are differences in instructional decisions made intuitively as contrasted with those using test information, or on the consequences of intuitive as contrasted with test-informed decisions. In addition, they report mixed evidence regarding the diagnostic-prescriptive teaching model, the model that seems most clearly to integrate assessment with instruction. The positive answers have come from researchers studying its use in the mainstream of education, the negative from those who have examined its use for special education (Rudman and others, 1980).

There is, however, some evidence that teacher understanding and use of tests is associated with improved pupil performance. Yeh (1978) found that staffs of schools whose children did poorly on educational measures were least likely to use test results; those where pupil performance was high, were most likely to use tests. And the more knowledge that teachers had about testing, the more they viewed tests as useful. These findings are remarkably consistent with reports from Denham and Lieberman (1980), emphasizing constant monitoring of pupil progress and high academic standards as two of the distinguishing features of more effective teachers and schools.

Such data and a durable belief in "the need today to make instructional decisions more rational and perhaps less intuitive" (Rudman, 1980, p. 4) have spurred efforts to understand why tests are widely administered but little used in schools for instructional insights, and to increase utilization.

## Increasing the Contribution of Achievement Tests to School Improvement: Classroom and Building Levels

Several developments offer considerable promise for increasing the contribution of achievement tests to school improvement; most are being tried in some schools and classrooms.

*Teaching/Testing Congruence.* The first development is the application of two strands of research, one showing that what happens in classroom *does* make a difference in student achievement and the other, the importance of test/curriculum congruence. As allocated learning time (ALT) and engaged learning time (ELT) increase, measured achievement in subjects taught during this time increases also. The relation of time-on-specific-tasks to measured achievement on related tasks has been reported in a number of correlational studies (for example, Denham and Lieberman, 1980). More compellingly, some but not all efforts to increase academic achievement through increasing ELT also have reported changes in student achievement as ELT has changed (for example. Holley and Ligon, 1980).

These effects are demonstrated most clearly in fine-grained analyses of test/curriculum congruence. Schwille and others (1981) and Freeman and others (1980), for example, have shown that differences in student achievement among teachers using similar curriculum guides in elementary mathematics depends on whether the multiplication taught involved two, three, or four place numbers if the tests used to assess learning also involved multiplication of two, three or four place numbers. He and his associates have found that the overlap between how instructional time is spent and items commonly used on norm-referenced tests to assess student achievement is as low as 25 to 30 percent.

In some school districts, knowledge of the consequences of this mismatch between norm-referenced tests and the curriculum is being applied in formulating instructional goals, allocation of instructional time, and selection of measures of achievement. From his experiences as Superintendent of Public Instruction for Illinois, Cronin reports: "The Valley View school district in Illinois was troubled by the fact that test scores locally were going down, despite the fact they had excellent staff, good programs, good leadership and new facilities. . . . They hired the Academy for Educational Development to come in to help them out. The first activity was to ask what congruence there was between the tests and the goals and objectives. They found the tests included about 40 percent of content that they weren't teaching. . . . A whole bunch of goals and objectives did not show up in the tests. So they looked for a test that had all these and the best had about 60 to 70 percent of their content, so they figured they could use sections of five or six tests. This is going to be really important in the future . . . not looking further at the tests themselves but at the activities of the classroom teachers, at the substance of curriculum, and instructional activity to find out if there is a match between them and the objectives on the one hand and between the output and measures on the other. . . . This one school district appears to have done it. Now they've got their tests to respond to their goals and they are working to get their teaching and practices and activity in line. They say that the scores are beginning to inch up slowly" (Millsap, in press). Similar patterns were found by Kennedy, Apling and Neuman: "One influence on the use of test results is the extent to which skills or knowledge tested happens to measure overlap with those the teachers' materials happen to cover. Of course, the match between these two instructional tools was not entirely haphazard, but the tests found most useful for instruction seem to be those that were keyed directly to the instructional materials" (1980, p. 94).

These views are echoed in the recommendation of the 1981 report on reading, writing and thinking of the National Assessment of Educational Progress (NAEP). Concluding that American schools have been successful at teaching students to formulate quick, short interpretations, the NAEP analysts recommend stressing writing in all curriculum areas; systematic writing instruction requiring explanation, interpretations, and critical thinking; instructional support of teachers in incorporating new writing and discussion tasks into the curriculum; in-service training on teacher writing and thinking systems; and changes in testing: "Tests are a direct reflection of what is valued by the school. If teacher-made tests as well as standardized examinations rely exclusively on short-answer formats, the message will be clear to teachers and students alike. Essay questions that require students to explain their points of view should be a regular part of any testing program" (National Assessment of Educational Progress, 1981, p. 4).

*New Information Technologies.* The second development offering promise of increased contribution by achievement tests is application of new information technologies to provide more rapid feedback on what children are learning. In its more widely used form, this means such devices as easily accessible cumulative files of pupil progress. In the more experimental mode, use of microprocessors to facilitate integrating instruction and testing is moved beyond the pilot phase in some districts.

McCormack, Assistant Superintendent of the Lawndale (California) school system, reported: "I use the printout with teachers. We have to teach the teachers how to read printouts and we repeat the training each year, sometime twice a year. . . . we've been using test results with teachers to help them see what needs to be stressed in the classroom. By looking at that data, there was no doubt about what was not being taught well. Our kids were marvelous at the beginning and ending of words. They never go to the middle vowels or the phonemes because the teacher had not clearly laid down the sequences of skills . . . decoding, comprehension, and interpretive skills—that are required to teach mastery in reading. . . . We improved our reading scores significantly in the second grade this year by making the teachers aware of what they need to emphasize" (Millsap, in press).

Prompt availability of test data, coupled with guidance on how to interpret and use it, at least in some school systems, seems to be making a difference.

Some operational projects are integrating closely testing and instruction. Charp (1979) indicates that computer assisted instruction has been used since 1968 in the Philadelphia schools, particularly for low-income students who need additional instruction in mathematics, reading comprehension, and decoding. In addition to the use of on-line tests for selection of initial difficulty levels for instruction and interspersed criterion tests, chapter tests, and multitopic tests, Philadelphia on-line systems include:

1. Programs individualizing not only the rate at which students pass through an instructional sequence but also the nature of the sequence itself by assessing reading level (0-2 years, 3-5 years, 6 years and above); aptitude level (below, average, or above); learning style (visual, auditory and kinesthetic) and cognitive style (abstract or concrete relationships). This particular system focuses on basic school objectives defined as minimal outcomes of middle schools (5 through 8) in mathe-

matics, science, social studies and communication arts. Student response to diagnostic and progress tests, together with initial sequencing information, influences what kind and sequence of learning activities are provided—a task often beyond the time available for most teachers without computer assistance.

2. Another set of programs maximizes options for student, computer and teacher interactions: as an example, after a student "signs on," the computer will administer a brief level verification test, the results of which are flashed on a teacher's display. The teacher has the option of skipping a student based on the pretest analysis to another module's pretest or to any unit within the current module. Skips over a pretest directly into another module are not allowed, so access to new modules is controlled by student progress.

A conceptually more complex scheme is under development by Schwartz and Taylor (1979) through Project Torque. Torque materials involve elementary level teaching of computation and measurement skills. Both have been field tested with 15,000 and more students, and both include tests, diagnostic manuals for teachers, administrative materials for teachers and administrators, and management packages. The Torque materials emphasize diagnosis of the reasons for student difficulties (as shown by the tests). They use, for example, constructed answers rather than selected answers; the diagnostic materials include a general description of the kinds of errors most frequently found on the tests and the specific wrong answers that may indicate these errors. Although Schwartz's work, and other diagnostically oriented programs such as those of Brown and Burton (1978) and of Davis and Henkin (1979) do not depend on computers to be useful, microprocessors may make feasible large scale use of these diagnostic and instructional modules.

*Increasing Appropriate Use.* Improving appropriate use of tests through better timing, better interpretive materials, and teacher training has been the primary strategy recommended by several groups concerned with testing and school improvement. Kean reported to a 1980 conference: "We are very very aware that no matter what we do in releasing test results, typically they do not serve the real needs of, or at least are not understood by, the primary clients (teachers, principals, and parents). So we are in the process of developing a creative communications package with several large test development firms, one of which has made a large resource commitment to the development of such a test package" (Millsap, in press).

While emphasizing the value of better constructed tests and tests which assess actual instruction, Rudman and his colleagues place greatest hope in linking the tests to teachers' instructional decisions, along the lines of Shavelson and Stern's (1981) studies of teacher planning. They argue: "Some significant and important decisions are made by the teacher early in the year (grouping, pacing, remediation, time allocations, subject area weakness and strength identification within a class) and all these decisions can be enhanced by proper utilization of information. . . . this is a critical point at which teachers could be reflective about their use of measurement concepts in their assessments, how these concepts relate to their instructional decisions, and about which concepts they would like further instruction" (Rudman and others, 1980, p. 10).

Their review of research on teacher knowledge of testing underscored the importance of training as well as timing. Teachers think they know more than they actually do. Olejnik (1979), for example, found that although over 90 percent of a sample of elementary and middle school teachers, counselors, and principals were at least somewhat confident of their ability to interpret test scores, 77 percent incorrectly assumed standardization and norms were the same, 65 percent did not recognize that a two stanine difference is significant, and 82 percent could not interpret properly a grade equivalent score.

The report of the 1978 national conference on achievement testing in schools (Tomlinson and Treacy, 1979), as well as the recommendations of the 1978 Falmouth conference (Tyler and White, 1979), stressed promotion of appropriate expectations about the uses and limitations of tests and testing. Interpretational materials provided by test publishers (alluded to by Kean and analyzed by Rudman and others, 1980), clearinghouse services aimed at classroom and building users of tests (such as the Center for the Study of Evaluation's testing and evaluation guides and the work of the Clearinghouse on Applied Performance Testing at the Northwest Regional Laboratory), and special reports, such as *Your Child and Testing* (Herndon, 1980), gradually may help demystify achievement testing, and prepare classroom and building educators for their instructional use.

*Minimum Competency Testing Program.* A fourth influence on use of tests at the classroom level are the minimum competency testing programs. It is too early to tell whether these programs will set a floor of instructional emphasis or a ceiling on achievement. Both advocates and opponents seem to agree (Herndon, 1981), however, that classroom teachers will take account of the instructional objectives explicit in the tests and foster the individual student's progress through these gates. Consider the classroom teachers testifying in the July 1981 Minimum Competency Test hearings (Herndon, 1981). According to Kathleen Gilbert, a fourth-grade teacher in Durham, North Carolina: "I know teachers who have planned vocabulary and math programs after copying the vocabulary and math items on the particular test achievement tests. I think allowing a test to determine our curriculum in this fashion has frightening implications. For instance, instead of the children getting lots of practice writing sentences and stories about personal experiences so that they learn to organize their thoughts and apply capitalization, punctuation, and grammar skills, they are reading an isolated sentence in a workbook and indicating which letters should be capitalized" (p. 23, day 3). Doris Hedgepath of Conway High School, Conway, North Carolina, viewed the impact more favorably: "one of the positive effects was more efficient use of class time for instruction. I feel that with this clear focus we are not wasting as much class time on items that perhaps we taught simply because we liked to teach them or felt comfortable with them. Now with this clear focus of a more standardized curriculum, I feel that we are making efficient use of class time. We are able to gear our teaching a little more efficiently for the individual's needs rather than the whole group's needs, and I think that is really where education is" (p. 35, day 1). Cumulatively, testimony at the Hearings (Herndon, 1981) indicate that the availability of improved methods for developing criterion-referenced tests, the widespread state testing programs, and competency based requirements for promotion and graduation are creating greater attention to—if not affection for—test use for instructional decisions at building and classroom levels.

In summary, while these four developments do not exhaust the probable influences on classroom and building use of achievement tests for instructional improvement, together they suggest that if Kennedy, Apling and Neuman were to revisit schools in about five years, considerably more utilization of test information for instructional decisions would be found among teachers and building principals, perhaps amid some debate on whether education, as a result, was better or merely different. Kennedy herself remarks, however, that this may be overly optimistic: "None of this addresses the teacher's fundamental preference for his or her own judgment. Where is there evidence that use increases with increases in technology, relevance of content, or timeliness of results?" (Personal communication, 1981).

## Use at District, State, National Levels Today

Participants at an October 1979 conference on education and assessment reported that the primary use of tests today is to make statements about the effectiveness of school programs and practices, and about schools, principals and teachers.

Blummer, Director of the New York City Office of Educational Evaluation, described testing activities within the City: "First among these, certainly the one that is most established and infamous in New York City, is the citywide achievement testing program, a testing program that results in a great media event every year with the publishing of the Rank Report of New York City Schools. Our elementary schools are ranked from 1 to 633, based upon the percentage at and above grade level, a procedure which all professionals in the system regard with abhorrence but which is mandated by the Decentralization Law. . . . . It is not a very useful way of informing the public of the effectiveness of activities within the school building, but I suspect that it is unfortunately perceived as useful by many" (Millsap, in press).

And Chase, considering local evaluations of federal programs, asserted: "the evaluation of federal programs has not been used very much to improve things in school districts. The evaluations are done to satisfy requirements so they continue to get the money" (Millsap, in press, p. 68).

McCormack, Assistant Superintendent of the Lawndale (California) School District, was similarly unenthusiastic: "My district is always going to be below the 50th percentile in the state ranking, always: we'll never be higher than that because our kids enter at the 17th percentile. That is what is published in the papers, and the school board asks me, 'How come we're always on the bottom of the pile?' " (Millsap, in press).

A similar perspective is given by Kennedy, Apling, and Neuman (1980). Many districts had a coherent attitude toward systematic information about changing enrollment, student behavior and tests performance; a consistent point of view about its relevance and appropriateness; and a recognized method for incorporating it into decisions.

The method, however, was other people's use: "Although many (district) administrators viewed test data as useful to others in improving instruction within buildings, they considered test data to serve themselves primarily in an oversight function, to be acted upon apparently only when evidence of a problem exists. . . . Many district administrators . . . used test scores to increase the accountability of principals or establish annual goals based on the test data; ranked buildings according to test data; or evaluated principals and teachers on the basis of test data . . . the rationale for all such policies was similar. For example, a superintendent in a small northern town said, 'The sight of the gallows shapes behavior' " (1980, p. 35). The researchers did not find that those who discussed testing relied on data in formulating policies. The function rather seemed that of a prod to force others to attend to the data, ". . . without substantiating the need to do so" (p. 37). "Their use of information was influenced in three ways: (1) that the issues with which they were struggling derived from a perceived change in status meant that data were used to monitor status, (2) the availability of descriptive data bases enabled policy makers to scan their environment and identify these status changes, and (3) the decision-making process influenced policy makers' use of information in that committees or other group strategies gave people time to adjust to the facts, opportunities to combine their personal knowledge with the facts, and opportunities to generate policy options that would accommodate both the facts and the political climate" (1980, pp. 44–45). At the national level, test use is similar. The reports of the National Assessment of Educational Progress, for example, which usually make headlines throughout the country, are descriptive, monitoring changes in status, rather than interpretative or prescriptive. And they usually are invoked, rather than interpreted, as causes of concern.

## Test Results as Prods

At the federal level, tests have been used in many evaluation studies. The Westinghouse evaluation of Project Head Start relied on the Illinois Test of Psycholinguistic Abilities as well as on specially constructed measures of reading and mathematics skills, attitudes toward school, and self-esteem (Cicarelli and others, 1969). The "disappointing" results, together with the "explanation" provided by Jensen's (1969) analysis of the heritability of intelligence contributed to holding Head Start funding level for a decade. Initial evaluations of the impact of Title I compensatory education programs involved administration of standardized reading and mathematics tests. The "disappointing" results, coupled with the "explanation" apparently provided by the study of *Federal Programs Leading to Educational Change* (Berman et al., 1974–78) supported expansion of technical assistance to local school districts as *the* strategy for program improvement. The national evaluation of Title VII (bilingual education) compared the reading and mathematics achievement of Hispanic children who had and had not participated in bilingual education programs (Damoff et al., 1978). Again, the disappointing findings together with emerging "explanations" of why such programs can't work are contributing notably to enthusiasm for approaches that have no component of instruction in the child's first language, even without compelling evidence in favor of these alternatives as instructionally more effective.

In these—and other instances— test results were used as prods. Alternative explanations of the results were reasonably abundant, yet few systematic efforts were made to sort out competing, plausible claims. They seem to have aroused attention, not because they were conclusive evidence of anything in particular, but because they didn't match expectations. The tests prodded people to rethink their assumptions about the relationships between practice and student performance. Eventually, a new climate of opinion emerged.

At the state level, perhaps the most striking example of this process is the spread of minimum competency testing programs as part of school improvement efforts. In half of the states—and school districts—where these programs have been adopted, performance at or above the cut-off score is necessary for high school graduation, but this is coupled with early identification and remediation in lower grades. The controversy surrounding minimum competency relies on expert judgment rather than on more systematic data to make the case for or against these programs. The substance of these debates suggests that there is a relatively loose connection between "the problem" of high school graduates who seem illiterate and minimum competency testing programs as a sensible educational solution. Some opponents in this case argue that many of the associated educational improvements—early recognition of children who are not progressing and heroic efforts to help them learn—are highly desirable, but decry the consequences of denying a high school diploma to the youth who still have been unable to make the cut score on the test. Other opponents assert that today's real problem isn't how to set a higher floor, but how to raise too low a ceiling, and that attention to maximum competencies—what they are, and how to get them—is more important. Again, the test findings were more prods to action than guides to well understood alternatives.

And at the local level, more than one school district has hailed the upturn of test scores in the elementary grades as proof of the efficacy of what the current superintendent has been doing, despite the availability of alternative interpretations, some of which point to other reasons, predict other changes, and lead to other actions. The rise in test scores reported by several large urban systems, for example, indeed could reflect the cumulative impacts of compensatory education programs many of which are competency based; it also could be due to greater stability of educational leadership and initiation of fewer new programs in recent years, when school closings have been among the greatest sources of turmoil locally. The rise also could be due to curricula and texts that have been created specifically for urban schools and which build on situations and vocabulary familiar to the children, or it could be due to rising levels of parental education and resources (in aid more than income), as well as the renaissance of some urban areas. Why do so many reports describing the percent of students passing (or failing) state competency tests, the college entrance examination averages, the National Assessment of Educational Progress results, or the ranking of local schools on yearly achievement tests seem to wave the scores as flags of distress or celebration, and then march forward prescriptively? (See, for example, Dearman and Plisko, 1981.)

Part of the reason is that most data permit little else, technically. An analysis of one widely cited finding—the so-called decline of comprehension scores on the National Assessment of Educational Progress tests—may illustrate this problem.

**Alternative Interpretations**

The National Assessment of Educational Progress in reading, writing and mathematics reports that, compared to the performance of seventeen-year-olds almost five and ten years ago, today's seventeen-year-olds are performing at lower levels than their earlier counterparts. The decline—for so it is described in most reports—does not appear, however, on factual and fairly rote items, such as spelling and vocabulary in reading, in grammar in writing, or computation in mathematics. It is most evident in tasks calling for comprehension, reasoning, and problem solving. Similar results have appeared on other achievement tests such as the College Entrance Examination Boards and in the reports of states and local districts which maintain similar data bases.

The problem is, what to do with these results. There are at least four interpretations of NAEP findings, which lead to different expectations of what the fifteen-year trends would look like and what to do about them. The first interpretation is that educational resources have concentrated on elementary grades and no one should be surprised if, lacking these extra resources, secondary schools aren't measuring up. This interpretation is plausible because some facts fit. Compensatory education money has concentrated by the millions on the elementary grades; so have curricular and teacher training attention. This interpretation predicts further *decreases* in test scores over the next five years, unless money and curricular attention are shifted to the secondary schools.

The second interpretation alleges that the past decade has seen the transformation of high schools into playpens for teenagers. Standards of student behavior and achievement have been set pitifully low, the schools lack serious purpose, and the curriculum lacks intellectual value. This interpretation, too, has the attractiveness of fitting some facts. High schools over the past decades have offered courses that may be more "relevant" but, except for the advanced placement programs offered in some schools, are not more academically demanding. High school graduation requirements in what are regarded as tough areas—advanced mathematics, hard sciences, classical and foreign languages—have gone by the board as colleges have dropped these as entrance requirements. High school is a way station, in terms of employment, not to a job but, for most youth, to community colleges and technical schools after which they enter the primary labor market. And the laxity of the curriculum is reflected in rapidly changing standards of conduct for youth, who are sleeping together earlier, having babies earlier, smoking more pot, drinking more beer, and generally raising more hell than even their parents. (See, for example, Cohen and Neufeld, 1981.) This interpretation, however, predicts *rising* test scores because the curriculum already is tightening up, and competency based exit requirements from high school are being matched by parental demands for more serious study as they have to pay more of the increasing bills for post-high school education. Continue these good works, this interpretation implies, and ye shall be rewarded by improved test scores.

There is, however, a third interpretation: the changes in the elementary school curricula that have led to rising test scores in the earlier grades may be at the expense of the thinking, reasoning, understanding, and comprehension skills needed for more complex work. We have sold our later conceptual birthright, if this be so, for a mess of higher, earlier scores on elementary grade tests which largely stress rote memory and routine calculations. "These findings seem to us a direct reflection of current emphases in testing and instruction in the classroom. The relatively short responses encouraged in classroom discussion parallel the multiple choice and fill-in-the-blank formats that dominate standardized and teacher-developed tests. When doing well in most school contexts requires little beyond short responses, is it surprising that students fail to develop more comprehensive thinking and analytic skills?" (National Assessment of Educational Progress, 1981, p. 2).

This interpretation, like the first two, fits at least some facts. The higher scores in the primary grades do seem associated with programs that emphasize direct instruction, often involving rote drill and practice, whose successes shine brightest when measured by similar items (Fenstermacher, 1979). Low and Wolfle (1981), for example, looked at the longitudinal effects of a particularly effective first grade teacher. Students of this effective first grade teacher did comparatively worse over the next several years. The interpretation was that the highly structured curriculum used by this teacher, which may prepare students to do well in the early elementary grades, did not give them the opportunity to develop problem solving and other higher order skills necessary for success in later grades. Many schools, though not all by any means, have shifted to these more structured materials, as reflected by the sales figures for the Sullivan Programmed Reading Materials and the rejection of the more cognitively based "new mathematics" curricula. In addition, recent research on the nature of skilled reading and skilled problem solving emphasizes the constructive quality of these activities. Many psychologists are calling for a revision of the early curriculum to restore these skills, as well as trying to remediate at the secondary levels the brains of students who have overdosed early on the wrong kind of successful program. This interpretation predicts *no change* in the test scores short of a fairly radical and long-term overhaul of the elementary school curriculum and a crash effort to learn how to remediate comprehension and problem-solving skills for youth who haven't learned them earlier. Efforts similar to these are in high gear already in the study skills and learning strategies courses offered in some school districts (for example, the Chicago and Fairfax school districts) and at community colleges and some universities. Internationally, Venezuela is urging developing nations to leap ahead of the industrialized ones, and to establish, as Venezuela has, Ministries of Intelligence.

And a fourth interpretation is that what we are seeing is a flow-through effect. The students who were the "lowest" group in the nine-year-old samples of ten years ago now form the "low" bar in the seventeen-year-old sample. The cohort who were the "middle" bar ten years ago, who remained in relatively the same position at their five year point, will become the upward swing in five years for the next seventeen-year-old sample, and the cohort forming in 1979–81 the highest bar that gives rise to rejoicing about the performance of the current nine-year-olds will flow through the system achieving at about the same levels. If we do nothing hastily counterproductive, according to this interpretation, these able learners—beneficiaries of whatever changes were associated with the upswing in test scores over fifteen years among the nine-year-olds—will continue to look good throughout their school careers. We can expect an *increase* if we don't do something, but stand there, without disrupting the schools and the country with unjustified hysteria about seventeen-year-old comprehension score declines.

There is little evidence on which the choice among these four interpretations can be made. They lead to substantially different paths of action or inaction, at substantially different direct costs.

**Prods into Plowshares**

Achievement related tests administered at district, state, and national levels for oversight purposes, as noted earlier, may involve more than trivial instructional opportunity costs as well as direct costs, with uncertain returns in instructional improvements. There are again some grounds for predicting improved use, based on current trends. It may be useful, however, also to consider an alternative.

**Current Trends**

Two current trends suggest wiser use of achievement test data for educational improvement. First, causal modeling techniques are being applied with considerable success to such large data bases as the Sustaining Effects Study. These techniques, which require advance specification of alternative hypotheses accounting for probable effects, are seen as alternatives to demonstration or experimental programs. Cooley has observed: "There are many problems with the experimental paradigm, including random samples not being available and the control of treatment not possible. As a result of these problems, many have turned to anthropology and the ethnographic approach. I have turned to sociology and economics where work in causal modeling has undergone substantial development during the past twenty years" (Millsap, in press). As an example of explicit causal models applied to educational data, Cooley continued: "Turning to the question of whether class size is correlated with student achievement in the primary grades, one cannot simply link the size of a student's class to her or his test score and compute the correlation at the student level. One must identify other factors related to class size, such as teacher experience, prior student achievement, a principal's policy to group low achieving students in small classes, and some teachers' decisions to allocate additional time for reading" (Millsap, in press). The experimental paradigm, as Cooley notes, while useful in many pilot testing situations (see, for example, Boruch and Cordray, 1981) is limited in its applicability to interpretation of large scale test data. Causal modeling techniques offer the discipline of systematic explication of the underlying model and identification of alternative explanations. They can lead to collection of targeted additional data (for example, teacher experience, prior student achievement). Examples seem scarce of applications of the causal modeling techniques to state and local achievement test data. Their utilization in the Sustaining Effects Study and Effective Schools project (Abt and Magidson, 1980) seem to be the most notable national applications, although internationally the techniques have been applied skillfully to such questions as the relation between literacy and productivity in developing countries.

The second trend is reduction in categorical programs, and the probable diminution of federally-generated pressures for compliance and accountability testing of children eligible for federal funds. When whatever testing is done to meet local and state needs, there may be greater opportunity to negotiate mutually useful information. Plato (1981) anticipates such benefits as a reprieve from multiple program requirements mandating unique program data collection and from the reporting necessary to keep programs in existence, possibly freeing resources for local evaluations, "potentially the best and most useful." Such a shift would be consistent with observations by Stecher and others (1981) on the local use of data. While resenting external pressures, local decision makers did use internally-generated data, particularly at the needs assessment/problem identification stage. Stecher and his colleagues argue for sharpening the distinction between information needed for satisfying external mandates and reporting, and data for local decision making, shifting responsibility for the latter to the building level evaluators, with technical assistance from district level evaluation and test specialists. "The capability for performing evaluation must be shifted to the local schools themselves" (p. 135). At least one school system has approximated such a model: in Atlanta, local evaluators serve small clusters of school buildings, collecting, analyzing and interpreting data aimed directly at helping principals and teachers improve school effectiveness. While Plato's (1981) analysis of the internal politics likely to be activated as a result of proposed budget reductions and program consolidation measures is an antidote to overly simplified predictions, the Atlanta approach at the least will provide a strong test of the analysis by Stecher and others (1981) of conditions under which test and evaluative data could lead sensibly to local school improvement.

The potential would remain, however, for uses of such remaining large data bases, as the National Assessment of Educational Progress, the college entrance examination reports, and state and local achievement testing as prods. What, if anything, might be done here?

## Time Out

Thinking through the meaning of data requires time. Almost an overload of data are available annually from achievement tests; often those responsible for collecting these data are absorbed—even before the reports of last year's data are written—in collecting next year's data and designing the study for the year after. It probably is no accident that the data bases which seem most thoroughly analyzed are those which are infrequent events: the national analyses by Coleman and others (1966) of equality of educational opportunity and, by Coleman and others (1981) of the relations among achievement, public, and private schooling. The achievement test scores which seem least fully understood through subsequent analyses, interpretations, and hypothesis testing (as distinct from attended to, lamented, or speculated about) are those which are annually available. The conferences on reasons for decline in achievement tests, for example, were more occasions for speculation, however wise, than of reexamination of data to rule out or confirm such alternative hypotheses as those illustrated for the NAEP findings.

How might one create conditions, then, favoring more thoughtful use of test data for school improvement on a federal, state or district scale? Caution would argue for offering no suggestions until the results on research in progress on local use of information from internal and external sources have been examined, competing interpretations identified, and if possible resolved through secondary analyses or additional data collection. Alkin, Cooley, Pechman, Kennedy and Banks (Gold, 1982) have collected a new, massive set of data on local use of internally-generated evaluation information and Louis and her colleagues (1981) have as remarkable a data base on local use of externally generated information.

In the spirit of adding to debate likely to develop as these and other (for example, Haggerty, 1918) data bases become more widely known, one possibility would be to establish longer intervals between testings. Such intervals might be dedicated, through reallocation of resources otherwise invested in collecting new data, to interpretation of the existing test results and formulation of strategies. In this sense, achievement test information might be used as something of a regulator of rate of educational change: collected more frequently when a sense of lethargy is considered a problem, less frequently when insufficient time for ideas to mature is seen as a problem.

Suggesting time out in across-the-board achievement test administration may seem regressive. For almost a decade, the results of neither standardized nor criterion-referenced achievement testing were acceptable to many school boards and scholars, particularly for low income and minority children. Such information seemed unjustly to have contributed to the belief that schools weren't teaching and children were incapable of learning. Only recently has the use of achievement test results to assess how well schools are doing returned to some general acceptability for urban schools. Concern that shifting from annual achievement testing to three to five year testing schedules could deprive the public of significant information on educational quality would be fair indeed in this context (Widgor and Garner, 1982).

Extending the period between testing for school accountability purposes need not interfere, however, with testing for the purpose of assessing individual student progress, with setting high standards of expectations, and with providing prompt feedback to teachers, students, and parents about individual student achievement. The likelihood that a single achievement test administered to all students in all grades in all schools of a state or large district will serve such individual purposes seems fairly small anyhow unless there is remarkable uniformity in what is taught from one class to another. Some combination of fine-grained, instructionally appropriate achievement tests and teacher observations is more likely to provide instructionally useful guidance for such individual decisions on pupil placement and progress.

Second, there are indicators of educational quality in addition to student test performance already influencing decisions, as Kennedy, Apling and Neuman (1980) show. Examining the instructional objectives and what is taught can be illuminating: schools offering little academic instruction and watered down content are unlikely to improve student achievement notably. Test data are scarcely needed for this kind of analysis. Attendance rates, completion rates, vandalism, and school safety are widely used indicators of school climate, of whether the school provides an atmosphere conducive to learning. Local teacher, parent, student, and community attitudes toward schools seem neglected but valuable sources of information on how well schools are doing. Less attention annually to test scores perhaps could contribute to greater attention to these indicators, some of which may have the additional advantage of suggesting more directly what changes might be instrumental to school improvement.

We have become accustomed to using legislation and funding as regulators of school change. Perhaps considering such a role for achievement test information, where frequency of administration is adjusted to the need for analysis of instructional strategies and the time required to implement changes will offer policy makers a useful additional resource for achieving educational improvement. This would recognize appropriately the valuable and dominant role achievement tests have come to play as the significant source of knowledge about the condition of teaching and of learning.

## References

Abt, W. P., and Magidson, J. *Reforming Schools: Problems in Program Implementation and Evaluation.* Beverly Hills, Calif.: Sage, 1980.

Anderson, B. L. "Test Use Today in Elementary and Secondary Schools." In A. K. Wigdor and R. W. Garner (Eds.), *Ability Testing: Uses, Consequences and Controversies.* Washington, D.C.: National Academy Press, 1982.

Berman, P., and others. *Federal Programs Supporting Educational Change,* Vols. I-VIII. Santa Monica: Rand Corporation, 1975-1978.

Boruch, R. F., and Cordray, D. S. *An Appraisal of Educational Program Evaluations: Federal, State and Local Agencies.* Evanston, Ill.: Northwestern University, 1980.

Brown, J. S., and Burton, R. R. "Diagnostic Models for Procedural Bugs in Basic Mathematical Skills." *Cognitive Science,* 1978, *2,* 155-192.

Charp, S. "Case Study: Instruction and Testing: School District of Philadelphia." In R. W. Tyler and S. H. White (Eds.), *Testing, Teaching and Learning.* Washington, D.C.: National Institute of Education, 1979.

Cicarelli, V., and others. *The Impact of Head Start: An Evaluation of the Effects of Head Start on Childrens' Cognitive and Affective Development.* Washington, D.C.: Clearinghouse for Federal Scientific and Technical Information, 1969

Cohen, K., and Neufeld, B. The Failure of High Schools and the Progress of Education. *Daedalus,* 1981, *110* (3), 69-90.

Coleman, J. S., and others. *Equality of Educational Opportunity.* Washington, D.C.: U.S. Government Printing Office, 1966.

Coleman, J., Hoffer, T., and Kilgore, S. *Public and Private Schools: A Report to the National Center for Education Statistics by the National Opinion Research Center.* Chicago, Ill.: University of Chicago, March 1981.

Damoff, M. *Evaluation of the Impact of ESEA Title VII Spanish/English Bilingual Education Program.* Volumes I, II, III, VI. Palo Alto, Calif.: American Institutes for Research, 1977-1978.

Davis, R. B., and Henkin, L. "Aspects of Mathematics Learning That Should be the Subject of Testing." In R. W. Tyler and S. H. White, (Eds.), *Testing, Teaching and Learning,* Washington, D. C.: National Institute of Education, October 1979, 60-81.

Dearman, N. B., and Plisko, V. "Test Scores and Attainment Rates," *American Education,* August-September 1981, 15-20.

Denham, C., and Lieberman, A. (Eds.). *Time to Learn,* Washington, D.C.: National Institute of Education, 1980.

Fenstermacher, G. D. "A Philosophical Consideration of Recent Research on Teacher Effectiveness." In L. S. Shulman (Ed.), *Review of Research in Education,* Vol. 1. Haska, Ill.: Peacock, 1979.

80

Freeman, D. J., and others. *The Fourth Grade Mathematics Curriculum as Inferred from Textbooks and Tests. Research Series No. 82.* East Lansing: Institute for Research on Teaching, Michigan State University, 1980.

Gold, N. *Proceedings of a Conference on Use in Schools of Locally Generated Evaluation Information,* January 1982. Washington, D.C.: National Institute of Education, in press.

Gorth, W. P., and Perkins, N. R. *A Study of Minimum Competency Testing Programs: A Report by National Evaluation Systems, Inc.* Washington, D.C.: National Institute of Education, 1979.

Goslin, D. A. *Teachers and Testing.* New York: Russell Sage Foundation, 1967.

Haggerty, M. E. "Specific Use of Measurement in the Solution of School Problems." In G. M. Whipple (Ed.), *The Measurement of Educational Products.* Seventh Yearbook of the National Society for the Study of Education, Part 2. Bloomington, Ill.: Public School Publishing Co., 1918.

Herndon, E. *Your Child and Testing.* Washington, D.C.: National Institute of Education, 1980.

Herndon, E. *Users' Guide: Minimum Competency Test Hearings.* Washington, D.C.: National Institute of Education, 1981.

Holley, F. M., and Ligon, G. D. *"Time: Today It Translates to Dollars."* Austin, Tex.: Office of Research and Evaluation, Austin Independent School District, 1980.

Houts, P. L. "Standardized Testing in America." *The National Elementary Principal,* 1975, *54* (6) 2-3.

Jensen, A. "How Much Can We Boost I.Q. and Scholastic Achievement?" *Harvard Educational Review,* 1969, *39,* 1-123.

Kellaghan, T., Madaus, G., and Airasian, P. W. *The Effects of Standardized Testing.* Dublin and Boston: St. Patrick's College, Dublin, and Boston College, 1980.

Kennedy, M. M., Apling, R., and Neuman, W. F. *The Role of Evaluation and Test Information in the Public Schools.* Cambridge, Mass.: The Huron Institute, 1980.

Louis, K. S. *Linking R & D with Schools: A Program and Its Implications for Dissemination and School Improvement Policy.* Washington, D.C.: National Institute of Education, 1981.

Low, L., and Wolfle, L. M. "Enduring Effects of First-Grade Teachers on Achievement." Paper presented at American Educational Research Association, Los Angeles, April 13-17, 1981.

Lyon, C. D., and others. *Evaluation and Decision Making in School Districts.* Los Angeles, Calif.: UCLA Center for the Study of Evaluation, 1978.

Millsap, M. A. (Ed.) *Towards Renewal and Reform: Evaluation and Testing in School Districts.* Washington, D.C.: National Institute of Education, in press.

National Assessment of Educational Progress. *Reading, Thinking and Writing: Results from the 1979-80 National Assessment of Reading and Literature.* Denver, Col.: Education Commission of the States, 1981.

Olejnik, S. P. "Standardized Achievement Program Viewed from the Perspective of Non-Measurement Specialists." Paper presented at annual meeting of the National Council of Measurement in Education, San Francisco, Calif., April 1979.

Plato, K. "Block Grants: Implications for State and Local Education Agencies." *Politics of Education Bulletin,* 1981, *10* (1), 6-9.

Resnick, D. P. "History of Educational Testing." In A. K. Wigdor and W. R. Garner (Eds.), *Ability Testing: Uses, Consequences and Controversies.* Washington, D.C.: National Academy Press, 1982.

Rosenshine, B. "How Time Is Spent in Elementary Classrooms." In C. Denham and A. Lieberman (Eds.), *Time to Learn*. Washington, D. C.: National Institute of Education, 1980.

Rudman, H. C. "Integrating Assessment with Instruction." Paper presented at an invitational conference on test use, National Institute of Education, Washington, D.C. June 1980.

Rudman, H. C., and others. *Integrating Assessment with Instruction: A Review (1922–1980)*. East Lansing: Institute for Research on Teaching, Michigan State University, 1980.

Schwartz, J. L., and Taylor, W. F. "Project Torque." In R. W. Tyler and S. H. White (Eds.), *Testing, Teaching and Learning*. Washington, D.C.: National Institute of Education, 1979.

Schwille, J., and others. "Teachers as Policy Brokers in the Content of Elementary School Mathematics." Paper presented at the February 26–28, 1981 NIE Conference on Teaching and Educational Policy, East Lansing, Mich.

Shavelson, R. J., and Stern, P. "Research on Teachers' Pedagogical Thoughts, Judgments, Decisions and Behavior." *Review of Educational Research*, 1981, *51* (4), 455–498.

Stecher, B. M., Alkin, M. C., and Flesher, G. *Patterns of Information Use in School Level Decision-Making*. Los Angeles, Calif.: UCLA Center for the Study of Evaluation, December 1981.

Tomlinson, T. M., and Treacy, M. E. (Eds.), *The National Conference on Achievement Testing and Basic Skills*. Washington, D.C.: National Institute of Education, 1979.

Tyler, R. W., and White, S. H. (Eds.), *Testing, Teaching and Learning*. Washington, D.C.: National Institute of Education, 1979.

Wigdor, A. K., and Garner, W. R. (Eds.), *Ability Testing: Uses, Consequences and Controversies*. Washington, D.C.: National Academy Press, 1982.

Yeh, J. P. *Test Use in Schools*. Los Angeles: UCLA Center for the Study of Evaluation, 1978.

Yeh, J. P. "A Survey of the Use of Various Achievement Tests." Paper presented at an invitational conference on test use, National Institute of Education, Washington, D.C., June 1980.

*Lois-ellin Datta is associate director, Program on Teaching and Learning, National Institute of Education.*

*The needs and aspirations of nontraditional college*
*students and of adult part-time learners call for*
*significant changes in educational programs.*

# Changing Student Populations

## K. Patricia Cross

Given the depressed and depressing atmosphere surrounding education these days, it may be necessary to remind ourselves that although the schools of the 1950s were widely admired and well supported, only half of the young people were staying in school through the twelfth grade. By 1964, the proportion had grown to two thirds, and by 1970, three fourths were graduating from high school. Boosting the high school graduation rate from 50 percent to 75 percent in just two decades is a phenomenal achievement, and it means not just more high school graduates but different kinds of students that reflect more accurately a cross section of the American public.

For higher education, the change followed a similar pattern; colleges extended the proportion of young people served from one fourth in 1952 to a third by 1964 to half by 1970. With increasing numbers came greater variety. In the competition of the 1940s and 1950s, colleges usually selected students who had already demonstrated that they were prepared to learn what colleges were prepared to teach. Today students select colleges; colleges are less and less likely to select students. Indeed, nation-

This chapter is an abbreviated version of a paper presented to the 1981 Summer Institute, Council of Chief State School Officers.

W. Schrader (Ed.). *New Directions for Testing and Measurement: Measurement,*
*Guidance, and Program Improvement,* no. 13. San Francisco: Jossey-Bass, March 1982.

wide, half of all students entering college today enter open-door community colleges.

Even before we get a good handle on learning how to teach more representative populations of young people, however, we are discovering that our task does not end with educating the *children* of all the people, but rather with educating all the people—many of whom are parents and grandparents. Because of the rapid escalation of educational attainment in recent decades, the reservoir of older people to be educated is exceptionally large at this particular time in our history. Never before, and probably never again, have the intergenerational differences in formal schooling been so great. Eighty-four percent of today's young people between the ages of twenty and twenty-four have completed four years of high school or more. Of their parents (ages forty-five to forty-nine), approximately two thirds have completed high school, but of the grandparent generation (ages seventy to seventy-four), only 38 percent have graduated from high school (U.S. Bureau of the Census, 1977).

Clearly, the individual of any age without a high school education or its equivalent is handicapped in making it in today's world where knowledge is exploding fast enough to create and wipe out entire industries within a single decade. People of all ages must, of necessity, become lifetime learners. No education will last a lifetime, and no educational program will be immune from constant change and evolution.

Two student populations seem to me most likely to require major change in the way we teach and structure education. For want of better terminology, I am going to label these two groups "basic skills students" and "adult part-time learners." Although no one seems to take offense at the labeling of adult part-time learners, the group that I am calling basic skills students has been subjected to a great variety of labels— disadvantaged, remedial, New Students, high risk, developmental, non-traditional, basic skills, and underprepared—to mention the labels in rough chronological order of their occurrence in the literature. I use the term *basic skills,* to suggest that these students are severely limited in choices because they lack the basic skills essential for lifelong learning. In an earlier era, they might not have graduated from high school and almost certainly would not have gone on to college.

## Basic Skills Students

My own research for the past decade has been concerned with describing the characteristics, motivations, needs, and interests of student populations newly aspiring to college, primarily poor students— economically and educationally—and adult part-time learners (Cross, 1971, 1976, 1981). In the studies of low achievers, I reanalyzed data from four large national data banks, ranging in size from 9,000 to 63,000 students, to compare attitudes, abilities, and interests of high school seniors scoring in the lowest third on traditional tests of academic achievement with those from the top third.

The lowest third I called New Students because they were "new" to higher education. I labeled the top third "traditional" students because the populations they represented had been going to college before the great explosion of open-admissions colleges in the 1960s. The majority of New Students are the white sons and daughters of blue-collar workers, although ethnic minorities are overrepresented among low-performing high school seniors. Whatever their color, New Students are typically first-generation college students. Neither they nor their parents know what to expect from college, but their hope is that it will lead to better jobs and greater choices in life.

I found highly significant differences between New Students and traditional students in self-concept, interests, and attitudes toward school (Cross, 1971). Young people who graduate from high school in the lowest third of the class look at education differently from those who have been more successful in school. They derive little satisfaction from their studies, and they are twice as likely as students in the top third to say that they feel tense, nervous, or shy in class. They rate themselves "below average" on almost any characteristic related to school work, agreeing, we might observe, with the teachers who have graded them throughout their school years. Community college teachers who have worked with these students in remedial education classes say that "low intelligence" is not the primary reason for their dismal school performance. Rather "lack of effort; has quit trying" seems to be the culprit (Cross, 1971).

It should surprise no one to learn that a young person, who proceeds through school a rather obvious failure at what is assumed to be the major job of young people, has given up trying when the result of effort rarely results in the teacher's reward of an A or in the admiration of peers. For the educational system, rooted in its traditions of semesters and the bell-shaped curve, there will always be a lower third. And that lower third will probably continue to think poorly of themselves and of school until they experience success as a result of their own efforts. That, I believe, is the major lesson learned from the research and experience of the past several decades. Our educational task, while enormously difficult and complicated, would seem to involve in some form the following ingredients: (1) to set learning tasks that are realistic for the individual, (2) to structure the tasks so that it is clear what is to be accomplished, (3) to maintain high expectations of performance, and (4) to provide the necessary help, but to permit students to reap the rewards of self-satisfaction as a result of their own efforts.

Both schools and colleges are incorporating these ingredients into programs designed to serve basic skills students. Because I am more familiar with programs in higher education than in secondary schools, however, I will comment briefly on the impact of these students on educational practices in higher education.

1. Most colleges and universities (81 percent according to Carnegie surveys) now have remedial programs in reading, writing, arithmetic, and other basic skills. Furthermore, such programs are almost as prevalent in selective universities as in community colleges (Stadtman, 1980).

2. Some form of individualization of instruction (for example, computer assisted instruction and video cassettes) is now offered in almost all (89 percent) institutions of higher education (Stadtman, 1980). Most colleges and universities, regardless of their admissions selectivity, have learning laboratories and learning specialists to help students at all levels of ability improve academic skills.

3. Diagnostic testing and placement are seen as increasingly important, and there is much less hesitancy to *require* students to take tests or remedial work than there was a decade ago. The permissive rhetoric of the 1960s that "students have a right to fail" has given way to the accountability rhetoric of the 1980s that "schools have an obligation to succeed."

4. Faculty are more articulate in defining needed competencies and more creative in using a greater variety of teaching methods. Furthermore, I see a growing number of college teachers who get their intellectual kicks out of tackling tough pedagogical problems.

5. Colleges are less easily intimidated by students who are unwilling to do the necessary work. Miami-Dade Community College, for example, is systematically raising expectations for remedial students, with reported increases in both student and faculty morale (McCabe, 1981).

**Adult Part-Time Learners**

Now let us turn to the second new student population that is exerting a major impact on education—adult part-time learners. Unlike basic skills students, who tend to be accepted reluctantly by educators, adult learners are desired and courted. Schools and colleges are finding themselves in fierce competition with one another as well as with other agencies of society for what is quite blatantly called "the adult market." It is estimated that about one in three American adults is engaged each year in some form of organized instruction.

To meet the demand, there are five leading providers of educational services for adults—community organizations, two-year colleges, four-year colleges and universities, employers, and grade and high schools—each with between 10 and 20 percent of the market. Employers and professional associations are also major providers of education for adults. It remains to be seen whether or how the balance will shift in the years ahead. There is a growing sense of unease over the organization and delivery of adult education, and providers who paid little attention to one another in more affluent days are now uncomfortably aware of the growing competition. Within universities, civil war is breaking out between extension divisions and the so-called main campus over whether services to adult part-time students should be decentralized into the various departments or centralized in extension divisions (Frandson, 1976).

There are also new turf wars between colleges that used to be friends; 80 percent of the institutions polled in a recent Carnegie survey admitted that they are experiencing competition from other colleges (Stadtman, 1980). In California, the competition between school districts and community colleges for adult programs resulted in a recent recommendation for binding arbitration in cases where turf fights cannot be settled amicably. Universities are finding themselves in big-time competition with professional associations such as the American Management Association and the American Institute of Certified Public Accountants, both of which have educational budgets running into millions of dollars (Stern, 1979). If educators are counting on their academic credit monopoly to win in the battle shaping up over adult learners, they can forget that advantage of an earlier era. Most adults don't care about academic credit, and many of the most prestigious adult programs, California's Continuing Education of the Bar or Harvard's Advanced Management Program, for example, carry no credit. Colleges seem to recognize that fact of adult life, and within the past ten years, more than a thousand colleges have newly entered the noncredit educational market.

If, however, adults do want credit for their learning, there are now plenty of ways to get it. Eighty-four percent of all colleges now grant credit for College-Level Examination Program (CLEP) tests (up from 35 percent in 1970); 41 percent grant credit by assessment of experiential learning (up from 14 percent a decade earlier) (Stadtman, 1980). Most also accept the credit recommendations of the American Council on Education's Office of Educational Credit for courses offered by employers or through the military services. In addition to having more options for college credit, adults can also choose among a new variety of degree-granting providers. Within commuting distance of my home in Boston are four new degree programs developed by agencies for whom education is a secondary activity—a consulting firm, Massachusetts General Hospital, a computer laboratory, and the American Institute of Banking. The degree offerings of these agencies range from associate to master's degrees. Indeed, there is so much going on so fast that traditional educators are finding themselves in a new intensely competitive and entrepreneurial ball game.

Frankly, I'm not sure what all this activity portends for the relationship between schools and higher education. The field is so much bigger than both of us that if we don't hang together we may very well hang separately. Perhaps the unique obligation that school and college educators share is that of helping students, whenever they are with us, become competent lifelong learners. That means several things.

First, we must teach, to the best of our ability, the basic skills that permit adults to continue to learn from a wide variety of opportunities. We have already spent considerable time on that issue, and I will not repeat the toughness of that assignment here.

Second, we need to promote the attitudes and values that contribute to an interest in continuous learning. There is already a sizable difference in the educational participation rate between the well-educated and the poorly educated, and that gap is growing. A college graduate is more than twice as likely to be engaged in adult education as a high school graduate, and a high school graduate is more than twice as likely as a nongraduate to be a participant. All studies of adult participation in educational activities show that the more formal education people have, the more interested they are in further education, the more they know about available opportunities, and the more they participate. In short, learning is addictive; the more education people have, the more they want and, of course, the better their position, politically and economically, to get what they want.

The worry is that there are many forces pushing in the direction of making adult education even more elitist than it already is. Many young professionals, for example, have little choice about continuing their education. States and professional associations are requiring members of certain vocations and professions to participate in continuing education in order to retain or renew their licenses to practice. Forty-five states require continuing education for optometrists, and a few states are setting up continuing educational requirements for *all* licensed vocations. Managers and young executives represent another group that is frequently under considerable pressure to gain further educational experience, either through employer-sponsored programs or through tuition reimbursement plans. In contrast, less well-educated people in the society are less likely to be pushed to participate; they are less likely to be paid or reimbursed for participation, and they are less likely to be given time off or employer encouragement. Thus, educational advantages and disadvantages have a way of piling up to create their own upward or downward spiral, toward or away from participation. Most studies show that a greater discrepancy exists between the well educated and the poorly educated on measures of *interest* than on measures of participation. The irony is that as new opportunities become available, the well educated will rush to take advantage of them while the undereducated will stay away in droves. At least that will be the case if the entrepreneurial mode continues to operate in which providers design and market their services to the most receptive markets.

Up to now, there has been a tendency for public policy to support educational programs for the economically and educationally disadvantaged. The problem comes in attracting adults who may have left school early precisely because they were unhappy and unsuccessful there. They are unlikely to return to learning programs that remind them of their early misery and embarrassment in school.

Formal education is surely the most critical part of the learning society. It develops the skills and forms the attitudes that make lifelong learning probable or improbable. As educators, we need to think more carefully about everything we can do to avoid creating a hard-core undereducated population that is alien to the new opportunities that are part of the learning society.

The third responsibility of formal education is to develop discerning consumers of lifelong education. It is a virtual certainty that adults in the twenty-first century will have an unparalleled choice of educational opportunities. They will need to know how to select the program that best meets their needs. That means knowing the advantages and disadvantages of the options available, but it also means knowing something about themselves as learners. I suggest that it should be a solemn responsibility of the compulsory school system as well as of higher education to teach students to be more self-aware of how they learn and which educational methods are working for them.

There is reason to think that the presence of a critical mass of discriminating learners in the society would stimulate the education industry in much the same way that gourmet cooks or physical fitness buffs have sparked remarkable vitality in the industries that serve them. Without question, knowledgeable cooks with developed tastes have stimulated the imagination and improved the quality of the cooking and dining industry. The more people know about foods, cooking, and nutrition, the more imaginative and responsive the industry must become. The gourmet cooking movement has demanded and received a tremendous response from restauranteurs, manufacturers of cooking equipment, cooking schools, and publishers of specialized cookbooks and magazines. A similar analogy can be made in certain sports. The more knowledgeable runners and joggers are regarding their needs, the more likely they are to demand forty varieties of running shoes over the all-purpose sneaker of a decade ago. Ten years ago, the sneaker industry would have said that there was no market for greater variety in active sport shoes. The difference between yesterday and today is that the society now consists of large numbers of runners and joggers and tennis players able to assess their individual needs and willing to pay large dividends to the industry responding.

In closing, I leave with you this question: Which came first, the demand for greater variety and sophistication in cooking equipment and running shoes or the imagination of producers and marketers who saw new needs and responded with creativity and imagination to first meet and then enhance the demand?

## References

Cross, K. P. *Beyond the Open Door*. San Francisco: Jossey-Bass, 1971.

Cross, K. P. *Accent on Learning*. San Francisco: Jossey-Bass, 1976.

Cross, K. P. *Adults as Learners*. San Francisco: Jossey-Bass, 1981.

Frandson, P. E. "Serving the Part-Time Student: Implications for Internal Mechanisms." *The NUEA Spectator*, June 1976, 43-45.

McCabe, R. H. "Now Is the Time to Reform the American Community College." *Community and Junior College Journal*, May 1981, 6-10.

Stadtman, V. *Academic Adaptations*. San Francisco: Jossey-Bass, 1980.

Stern, M. R. "Competition in Continuing Education in the 1980s." *AAHE Bulletin*, *32* (4) 1979, 3-4, 16.

U.S. Bureau of the Census. "Educational Attainment in the United States: March 1977 and 1976." *Current Population Reports*, series P-20, no. 314. Washington, D.C.: U.S. Government Printing Office, 1977.

*K. Patricia Cross is visiting professor, Harvard Graduate School of Education.*

*Efforts to improve instruction should place greater*
*emphasis on institutions serving the less advantaged.*

# Institutional Change:
# Remarks on Chapters by
# Datta and Cross

## Marshall S. Smith

Both Datta and Cross have set out arguments which suggest the need for modest changes in our schools and colleges. Cross's chapter addresses three goals for colleges to prepare people to be lifelong learners. Datta proposes ways of using test scores to prod school administrators and teachers to look for ways of improving the quality of schooling.

By saying that these ideas have only modest implications for change, I don't mean to be critical. The times may demand modesty in most instances to recapture the stability, sense of direction, and purposefulness that many saw the schools and colleges as losing during the late 1960s and 1970s. I am not convinced, however, that only modest change is needed for at least one segment of the school-age population. I will return to this point at the end of my discussion. Before that—and in the spirit of the two chapters—I will make some modest remarks on each of them.

Datta considered the causes of and implications for change of the test score decline. She argued that of the many possible causes, four stand out. However, she went on to say that we haven't been able to choose among the four causes and, since different actions follow different interpretations of cause, we don't know what action to take. Consequently, she

W. Schrader (Ed.). *New Directions for Testing and Measurement: Measurement,*
*Guidance, and Program Improvement*, no. 13. San Francisco: Jossey-Bass, March 1982.

suggested that local and state school administrators should routinely collect and examine data to try to evaluate possible interpretations in much the way that Freda Holley did in Austin, Texas. She seems to be proposing small, carefully designed, yet speedily conducted, studies that would examine specific hypotheses to explain increases or decreases in test scores. The studies could look at such variables as time spent on instruction, the diversity of school offerings, and student behavior in areas like homework and work for pay, all of which are prominent in the literature as having effects on student achievement. It is a nice proposal much in line with recent thinking about formative evaluation and research. We must realize, however, that many school systems lack the capacity to do the data collection and analysis necessary to carry out such studies. Three other thoughts occurred to me as I read her chapter.

First, it seems extraordinary that there have not been dozens of high-quality studies carried out to evaluate specific "causes" of the test score decline. The widespread nature of the decline, the tremendous amount of press it has received, the availability of many bodies of test score data—all would have suggested that the field was ripe for analysis. Yet since the Wirtz Commission report, there have only been a few attempts that I have seen to examine this particularly critical question. Perhaps the conclusion that there are multiple causes that are difficult to assess, when coming from a prestigious panel, has tended to depress the appetite for further examination rather than stimulate it. This is unfortunate for, as Datta points out, different causes may lead to important differences in consequences.

Second, turning to Datta's discussion of the causes and their implications, I see causes one and two—the past emphasis on improving early schooling and the present and future need for emphasis on later schooling—as being so similar as to be easily grouped together. If so, and one accepts the premise that many high schools are changing—becoming more structured, emphasizing academic curriculum more, asking for more homework—then her implication is that we don't need to intervene. Since explanation four—the "flow-through" one—leads to the same implication, we are left only with the third cause as implying anything other than inaction.

Recall that explanation three relates to the lack of attention that schools have given over the past fifteen years to teaching complex skills of analysis and comprehension and the impact of this on test scores starting in grades 4 and 5 and continuing through the end of high school. My own view of this explanation is that it fits the data better than the others and that it deserves immediate attention. Indeed, a good part of the effort at the National Institute of Education that Datta directs is aimed at exploring ways of changing this emphasis. One focus for attention might be the content of early grade achievement tests, which tend to provide reinforcement for curricula that place an emphasis on the narrow basics. In combination with the minimum competency tests, which in many states ask for little thinking and analysis from students, these early grade tests are an area where the content of the tests may be having a particularly detrimental effect on the content of the curriculum.

This leads to a third thought—we might be able to design tests that would help in our effort to determine some of the possible causes for increases or decreases in levels of achievement of schools or school systems. Items might be constructed to assess changes in the way that home background affects achievement. Other items might assess the relative emphasis on narrow cognitive skills versus reasoning and analysis in the curriculum. Such tests would be diagnostic of the needs of the school or system rather than needs of a particular student.

Let us turn now to the second chapter. I want to make only two brief comments that specifically focus on Cross's chapter.

First, her remarks on the obligation of schools to work with the lower third of the students are important. The expansion of special programs in institutions over the past fifteen years is extraordinary. Having looked for years for justification to improve federal support for these programs, however, I have considerable skepticism about their effectiveness and wish that she and others would pay far more attention to their evaluation and improvement.

Second, it may be heretical, but I remain skeptical about whether the nation is engaged in a rush to *lifelong education*. There have been great increases in college rates of attendance since the 1950s and early 1960s. Clearly also, people in the society are often more able to afford to pay tuition than in the past. Yet if we look at data on college enrollment for ages twenty-two to thirty-four over the past ten years, we find that the rate of participation for men has dropped—during a time when the percentage of men in the armed forces dropped dramatically. The small increase in total participation for the past decade is completely accounted for by increases in the number and percentage of women, and this seems to have leveled off.

Moreover, as far as I know, no one has successfully looked at the changing attendance patterns between such educational groups as the local church or YMCA and the more formal educational settings. I wonder whether we simply have a switch in place rather than an increase in rate of participation.

And, while it is clear, as Cross says, that certain professionals such as optometrists are requiring continuing education, this is not a particularly large part of the society. Contrast this with the findings about the apparent lack of interest of union employees in attending classes, even though their tuition is reimbursed by their employer.

Finally, if one believes the data on television watching, I can't see when people get the time to go to school.

As a naive observer, it appears to me that the apparent increase is mainly in circumstances where a clear reward such as a certificate or a new job follow course attendance or where the location is particularly convenient and the person is financially able to pay tuition. This observation is consistent with Cross's worry that continuing education may become more and more the prerogative of the wealthy. It also implies that institutions of higher education ought to be very careful as they invest in attracting these particular new students.

Finally, in both chapters the problems of the poor and low-scoring in the cities were only indirectly addressed. Cross did discuss the growth of community colleges, but this leaves out many potential students. She noted that "Up to now, there has been a tendency for public policy to support educational programs for the economically and educationally disadvantaged." One reaction to this is that the times are changing and public policy might also change. Another observation is that on balance, the statement has never been accurate. Federal policy and the policy of a few states, perhaps, have supported such programs—but *public policy, no*. This nation spends, out of tax dollars, up to eight times the amount on the advantaged half of the population that attends college as they do on the disadvantaged half that does not. Most of this comes from publicly subsidized tuition and costs at our big public colleges and universities. This is a dramatic imbalance in favor of the wealthy.

A second indicator of the lack of national interest in this population is the destruction of the CETA (Comprehensive Employment and Training Act) Youth Program during the past year. This has removed support for many community based organizations that were often the only institutions offering educational opportunities for youth who had dropped out of school.

This prevailing policy fits with the apparent lack of commitment of the nation to reduce the plight of public junior and senior high schools in the inner cities. Modest and rational strategies such as those suggested by Datta won't go far to improve most of these schools. Indeed, their condition, partly indicated by test scores, has motivated many people to move away from cities or to propose vouchers and tax credits for private schools.

Dramatic institutional change would be necessary to meet this problem—a topic which goes far beyond the boundaries of this conference. In the context of the conference, however, I do have a modest idea. The idea arose during the recent debates about the Youth Act of 1980. It combines two observations. First, competency tests are often seen as having little relevance to the "real world," and thus students see little reason to work hard to pass them. Second, employers often claim they don't hire blacks, Hispanics, and other poor people because they cannot read or write, even though they may have passed a competency test or graduated from high school. Frequently, in my view, this claim of employers serves as an excuse, which allows them to discriminate. A way to eliminate both the opportunity to discriminate and employers' legitimate arguments that some applicants are illiterate might be to give the employer a say in determining the content and skill levels required to pass the minimum competency test. In conversations with employers, there was general agreement to at least try such a strategy. Consequently, under the guidelines of the Youth Act, an employer would not have been able to reject a student applying for certain prespecified jobs for lack of basic skills if the student had passed a basic skills minimum competency test that the employer had participated in developing. The trick was to tie together the test with the promise of a concrete outcome like a job. Unfortunately, the idea seems to have died with the Youth Act.

Both presenters concluded with upbeat statements—Datta about the prospects for school improvement at the elementary and secondary level and Cross about the capacity of institutions of higher education to improve. I think this optimism is justified for the institutions serving the more advantaged. I wish I could say the same for the other half.

*Marshall S. Smith is professor of educational policy studies and educational psychology, Center for Educational Research, University of Wisconsin–Madison.*

*The age-in-grade, Carnegie unit lockstep basis for organizing schools is impairing the quality and extent of learning, especially for the ablest students.*

# Identification of Intellectual Talent

## *Julian C. Stanley*

In 1921 in California, systematic seeking for large numbers of intellectually talented youths began with Terman's somewhat unfortunately titled *Genetic Studies of Genius*.[1] His 1,528 school-age subjects born, on the average, in 1910 are considerably less numerous today, but as recently as 1972 the survivors were still being followed (Sears, 1977; Sears and Barbee, 1977). From this classic descriptive longitudinal study has come empirical refutation of most myths about intellectually talented youths. They do not tend to die early, peter out, burn out, become neurotic or psychotic, or fail in their professional and personal lives. Although the extent and quality of the contributions of Terman's "geniuses" (or Termites, as some preferred to call themselves) are still being debated, even in the 1960 survey their vocational achievements are impressive. While the group averaged only fifty years of age then, "Three men had been elected to the National Academy of Sciences and two to the American Philosophical Society. [Forty-six] are included in . . . *Who's Who in America*, ten in *The Dictionary of American Scholars*, and eight-one in *American Men of Science*. . . . Some 2,500 articles and papers and more than 200 books and monographs in the sciences, arts, and humanities have been published and at least 350 patents granted. Miscellaneous articles (technical, travel, hobby, and so on) number around 350. Other publications include close

W. Schrader (Ed.). *New Directions for Testing and Measurement: Measurement, Guidance, and Program Improvement*, no. 13. San Francisco: Jossey-Bass, March 1982.

to 400 short stories, 55 essays and critiques, and a small amount of poetry and several musical compositions. Not included in the foregoing account are the professional output of editors and journalists or the many radio, television, and motion picture scripts that have been authored" (Oden, 1968, pp. 19–20).

Oden goes on to discuss contributions of architects, artists, and musicians in the sample. Though less extensive than the verbal output, their productivity is fairly impressive to persons who do not demand a Picasso or Mozart from a relatively small number of high-IQ children in a single state during a growing-up period that spanned the depression-ridden 1930s.

The persistent reporting of findings in four volumes, a mono-graph, and many articles did much to quell the worst fears of the unin-formed prejudiced. Being almost solely a nonmanipulative study of the gifted child in his or her native habitat, however, this great work had little to say, except incidentally, about educational facilitation of high-IQ stu-dents. Also, because during those early days he dealt primarily with a global measure of intellectual ability, Terman told us little about specific intellectual talents and how they might be useful educationally. This led teachers to group children for instruction in many school subjects by IQ, rather than on the basis of whatever combination of abilities best pre-dicted success in a given course. That may explain a considerable part of the failure of homogeneous grouping, ability grouping, and streaming. For example, grouping in IQ reduces the variability of mathematical reasoning ability within the group far less than grouping on mathemati-cal reasoning ability itself would.

Concurrently with Terman, but at Teachers College of Columbia University in New York rather than at Stanford University across the country, Hollingworth (1942) both identified and facilitated education-ally a considerable number of extremely high-IQ children. Terman worked for the most part from IQ 140 up, whereas Hollingworth pre-ferred at least 180. Her methods were less surveylike and more personal than his. Despite her untimely death in 1939 at age fifty-three, she has had a continuing impact on the education of the gifted. Her emphases on special schools for them and moderate educational acceleration affected the New York City area, especially during the 1920s and 1930s, and quite a few other large cities. Like Terman, however, she emphasized the single-score, Binet-type IQ for identification and educational placement.

A third towering figure was Pressey (1949). He and others (for example, Worcester, 1956; Hobson, 1963) sought freedom for intellectu-ally able youths to traverse the school system from kindergarten through graduate school faster than the usual age-in-grade, Carnegie-unit lock-step. Going beyond Terman and Oden (1947) and Hollingworth (1942),

Pressey showed that the presumed evils of educational acceleration were about as imaginary as had been those alleged for having a high IQ.

Many others have worked on some aspect of great intellectual ability, from Galton (1869) to the present, but during the fifty years from 1921 until 1971 Terman's research-oriented talent search remained virtually unique. It did, however, inspire a number of states—notably, California—to search systematically for high-IQ youths and provide them with some special provisions, chiefly what came to be known as educational enrichment (Kearney and Brockie, 1978).

## Study of Mathematically Precocious Youth

My interest in general intellectual talent was kindled by a course in tests and measurements at the University of Georgia during the summer of 1938. At that time I was a barely twenty-year-old veteran of a year of teaching in as nearly a blackboard-jungle high school as Atlanta could provide. Much of that summer course consisted of the students' taking a number of intelligence tests, notably the Otis, Toops' Ohio State University Psychological Test, and the Miller Group Test, one third of which later grew to become the Miller Analogies Test. For a year or so I administered the Otis to everyone who could be persuaded to take it, including my students, my parents, my girl friends, and my sister's boy friends. I even went on to administer a standardized chemistry achievement test to my high school chemistry class. This testing was heady experience, but other concerns such as the coming world war took over. Not until 1958 did my interest in gifted children resurface, but then it gave way to a Fulbright year abroad devoted to test theory.

In 1971 a fortunate combination of events led to my securing a generous grant from the newly formed Spencer Foundation of Chicago. It provided a decade of support, still continuing, for an ever-growing annual talent search among junior high school students. Unlike Terman's, however, this search was conceived from the start as a means of finding youths with special talents who could be helped to move ahead better and faster educationally. Terman and Pressey had provided powerful ammunition against most of the worst stereotypes; strong, determined educational facilitation was needed. It is not possible, however, to facilitate unknown or imprecisely identified youths (Stanley, 1976). Efficient searching was clearly the initial step, necessary but not in itself sufficient.

The first search was conducted in March of 1972 with 450 seventh and eighth graders, chiefly from the Baltimore area (Stanley, Keating, and Fox, 1974). By January of 1981, the eighth search involved 14,676 seventh graders from six Middle Atlantic states and the District of Columbia, plus some 11,000 students in the Southeast and West under the auspices of Duke University and Arizona State University, respectively.[2] During the present school year about thirty-three states will be firmly in the talent-search network, with them and most of the others being canvassed more lightly for ultra-high-level talent. The searching has grown large and complicated, but effective, because of the accumulation of relevant experience during the decade. As might be expected, facilitation efforts have also been expanded greatly.

From the start, the chief identifying instrument used by my Study of Mathematically Precocious Youth (SMPY) was the College Board's Scholastic Aptitude Test (SAT). At first chiefly the mathematical part (SAT-M) was administered, because SMPY wanted mainly to find and help young students who reason extremely well mathematically. Soon, however, values of the verbal part (SAT-V) became apparent. Searches from number seven onward are as much for verbal reading and reasoning ability as for mathematical reasoning ability. Even the Test of Standard Written English (TSWE) has proved useful for determining readiness for foreign language and writing courses.

Fears that youths eleven to thirteen years old would find the SAT too difficult have not proven true, probably chiefly because we restrict participation in the talent search to persons who, on achievement-test batteries administered by their schools, score in the top 3 percent of their group verbally, mathematically, or overall. Thus only about one in twenty seventh graders or youths in higher grades who are not yet thirteen years old qualify for the talent search. The abler of these tend to be the ones who actually take the SAT, so for the most part the Johns Hopkins Office of Talent Identification and Development (OTID) deals with the top one in thirty or so youths. Interest focuses on those who score at least 500 on SAT-M or 430 on SAT-V. By comparison, the average college-bound, twelfth-grade male scores 492 and 430, respectively. To score that well five years earlier than high school seniors represents considerable intellectual precocity and, other factors being favorable, potentiality for accelerating one's progress in relevant school subjects.

How do eligible students learn of OTID's annual talent search? Full explanatory materials concerning it are sent independently to four different educators at every public, parochial, and independent school in the Middle Atlantic Region that has a seventh grade. Also, extensive news coverage is sought in this geographical area (Delaware, District of Columbia, Maryland, New Jersey, Pennsylvania, Virginia, and West Virginia). The student need learn from his or her school only about the upper-3 percent score on a relevant part of an in-school achievement-test battery. The eligible student then registers directly with OTID, which in turn sends information about preparing to take the SAT in January and much other material.

Scores from the January SAT testing come to OTID via its code number, at which time (usually mid to late February) supplemental information concerning summer programs is sent to all the examinees whose SAT scores qualify them for such fast-paced academically oriented experiences. For example, of the 14,676 participants in OTID's January of 1981 talent search, 1,378 scored high enough on SAT-M to become eligible to attend the concentrated three-week residential precalculus program that summer.

## National Search for Super Talent

In the fall of 1980, SMPY started a national search for youths who score at least 700 on SAT-M before their thirteenth birthday. Only 5 percent of college-bound, twelfth-grade males score that high. We estimate that at a given time only 350 to 500 persons in the country do that well before age thirteen, making them the top 1 in approximately 10,000 of their age group. This one hundredth of 1 percent mathematical reasoning ability holds promise of stellar academic performance, especially in the mathematical and physical sciences and engineering, all the way through the Ph.D. degree at a top-level university. This precious natural resource was seldom discovered before we went looking explicitly for it. Truly, youths of this quantitative caliber were "born to blush unseen, and waste [their] sweetness on the desert air"[3] of elementary and junior high schools. At age twelve or thirteen the majority of them could dispose of the usual four-and-one-half-year precalculus sequence from first-year algebra through analytic geometry well in three intensive summer weeks, thus becoming ready for twelfth-grade Level BC Advanced Placement Program calculus when just eighth graders, rather than only for Algebra I in the eighth or ninth grade. How much boredom and frustration they were spared by being identified objectively by means of a well-known, secure instrument—SAT.

From November of 1980 until the last SAT testing that school year, in early June of 1981, SMPY found sixty-three with scores of 700 or better on SAT-M before age thirteen. Twenty-three of these came through OTID's January of 1981 talent search, four through Arizona State University's Project for the Study of Academic Precocity (PSAP), two through Duke University's Talent Identification Program (TIP), and the remaining thirty-four through SMPY's national publicity, chiefly in newspapers. As a response of the estimated 350–500 such youths in the population, this was gratifying for a first effort. Even though some of the sixty-three were found too late for admission to the summer programs conducted by Johns Hopkins or Duke, and despite the fact that three of them were already full-time college students and therefore not in need of those classes, forty-seven attended at least one three-week session and three attended both. SMPY continues its contacts with these remarkable young students in the fall as they try to articulate their summer educational accomplishments with the curricula of the schools (mostly public ones) they attend across the country. Also, it awaits a new group when SATs are again offered.

This special talent search is conducted simply. Any interested youth may secure from a senior high school a copy of the official SAT practice booklet, entitled "Taking the SAT," study it, take the test, and, if the score is at least 700, send a copy of the score report to SMPY, Department of Psychology, Johns Hopkins University, Baltimore, Md. 21218. An examinee may qualify up to age thirteen and almost ten months with an 800; for every month or fraction of a month past the thirteenth birthday, 10 more points are required on SAT-M. For example, at age thirteen and nearly three months, a score of 730 or more is needed. Obviously, we are estimating that just prior to his or her thirteenth birthday the score would have been at least 700. This rough procedure is needed because the SAT is not offered every month of the year, with an especially large hiatus during the summer and early fall.

OTID is launching a similar search for verbal superstars, those who before age thirteen score at least 630 on SAT-V. (630 is the 95th percentile of college-bound, twelfth-grade males). Students may qualify, with a score of 800, even as old as fourteen years and less than five months—10 points beyond 630 for each month or fraction of a month beyond the thirteenth birthday. Score reports at that level should be sent to OTID, at Johns Hopkins University.

**Sex Differences on SAT-M**

Even though extremely able mathematical reasoners were sought across the country in many ways, all sixty-three that we found are male. This complete lack of girls is surprising for at least two reasons: (1) Of the approximately 16,000 females in the eight SMPY and OTID talent searches thus far, 7 (found in the fifth, sixth, and seventh searches) scored at least 700 before age thirteen; the ratio of boys to girls is 17:1 over all talent searches, not the 63:0 of the recent search. (2) Several girls scored almost 700 well before their thirteenth birthdays. One of them scored 690 when only ten years old. Therefore, some girls will qualify soon.

How do the boys who score this high on SAT-M differ from the girls who do? Three of the seven girls are of Asian background, two being Chinese-American and the other Japanese-American. Eight of the sixth-three boys are of Asian background: four Chinese-American, two Korean-American, and two Indian-American. Another boy is Guatemalan, apparently of Spanish, Indian, and Chinese ancestry. These figures suggest considerably greater representation of Asian-background youths than their proportion in the national population. Also, a sex difference in Asian background is suggested, but with only seven girls it cannot be estimated reliably. Of course, in this talent search one cannot separate the effects of volunteering from those of differences in mathematical reasoning ability of various ethnic groups.

As Table 1 shows, the SAT-M scores of the seven girls ranged from a 700 to a 780, with a median of 750. It appears appropriate to compare the SAT-Verbal scores of the six U.S.-born girls with those of the sixty-two U.S.-born boys.[4] These six girls' SAT-V scores ranged from a 530 to a 750, the lowest and highest scores both by Chinese-Americans. Their median was 685; five of the six girls scored at least 640, whereas only nine of the sixty-two boys scored that high.

The boys also ranged from 700 to 780 on SAT-M, but, unlike the girls, tended to be concentrated near the minimum qualifying score. The median of their SAT-M scores was 720. On SAT-V they varied from 310 (and 760M) to 750 (and 720M), the median being 530. Whereas only 17 percent of the six girls scored verbally below the 96th percentile of college-bound, twelfth-grade males, 87 percent of the sixty-two boys did. On college-bound, twelfth-grade male norms, four of the six girls were at least as able verbally as mathematically, whereas only five of the sixty-two boys were. (630V has the same percentile rank as 700M, and only nine of the boys scored that high on the verbal tests.)

Given the obviously severe limitation in the size of the sample of girls, these data nevertheless suggest for further study the possibility that nearly all girls who score extremely high on SAT-M do so mainly because they are brilliant verbally, whereas quite a few boys exhibit what appears to be strong dependence on the nonverbal hemisphere of the brain. Do such boys have greater aptitude for learning mathematics through elementary college calculus and differential equations than most verbally superb girls? Perhaps their aptitude for more abstract mathematics such as analysis, higher algebra, number theory, and topology is less than the girls'. If so, girls like these may face the dilemma that they perform less well in algorithmic mathematics and are less interested in it than they would be in "purer" mathematics. Admittedly, this is highly speculative. Fortunately, the conjecture is subject to various empirical tests, especially at SAT-M levels such as 600, where a larger number of females can be secured. Benbow and I (Benbow and Stanley, 1980, 1981; Benbow, 1981) have calculated male-to-female sex ratios of seventh and eighth graders at 500 up (2:1) and 600 up (5:1), but have not yet studied M versus V discrepancies within those groups.

Sex differences in mathematical reasoning ability as ascertained from SAT-M and similar tests are large enough to be important. In my opinion, they warrant sound study to ascertain why they occur and what implications they might have for amelioration and instruction. It serves no useful purpose to deny the existence of such differences. The "whats" are rather clear, but of course the "whys" are not. Talent searches such as those described here provide excellent opportunities for much-needed research.

## For the Future

As I (Stanley, 1977) have argued, SAT-M was a virtually ideal instrument for the Study of Mathematically Precocious Youth (SMPY) in its formative stages. Youths who reasoned extremely well mathematically were found and then studied further in many ways (Stanley, Keating, and Fox, 1974; Keating, 1976; Stanley, George, and Solano, 1977; George, Cohn, and Stanley, 1979; Fox, Brody, and Tobin, 1980; Benbow and Stanley, in preparation). SAT-M, SAT-V, and TSWE continue to serve SMPY's and OTID's initial identification needs well. For finding more varieties of intellectual talent, however, a comprehensive aptitude-test battery might be developed by the College Board for use in the early years of junior high or middle schools. This might be administered to the intellectually ablest 5–10 percent of the age group in a search for persons highly apt in one or more of at least half a dozen societally valuable intellectual ways. Business, industry, and the professions need more than mathematical and verbal reasoning ability and knowledge of the mechanics of English expression.

For example, most of the nation's schools give little attention to the need for skilled maintainers of technical hardware whose excellence in mechanical reasoning, nonverbal reasoning, and spatial relationships has been utilized from the early years to make them highly proficient. Seldom do educators even know who the young students scoring extremely well in these respects are or care much about their special abilities if they do. Many potentially splendid repairers of copying machines, computers, electronic musical instruments, plumbing, and automobiles become routine service persons or mediocre engineers instead. Often, persons who perform poorly in academic subjects are shunted to the semiskilled or skilled trades by default, rather than because they have the requisite aptitudes for them. The first step toward alleviating this unfortunate situation is to call attention to the large pool of mechanical, spatial, and nonverbal reasoning ability. This could probably be accomplished best by a comprehensive national talent search at the upper elementary or junior high school level. The College Board and ETS are eminently qualified to conduct it.

## Reorganizing the Educational System

Identifying intellectual talent objectively is the necessary, but hardly sufficient, condition. As some wag quipped, "You can't major in IQ." Mental potentiality is merely an aid to learning. The quality and

Table 1. Frequency of SAT Scores of 700M or More Before Age Thirteen
for Boys (B) and Girls (G)

| Score Scale | $M^a$ B (63) | $M^a$ G (7) | V B (62) | V G (6) | $TSWE^b$ B (62) | $TSWE^b$ G (6) |
|---|---|---|---|---|---|---|
| 780 | 3 | 1 | | | | |
| 770 | 1 | | | | | |
| 760 | 4 | 2 | | | | |
| 750 | 6 | 1 | 1 | 1 | | |
| 740 | 3 | 2 | | | | |
| 730 | 10 | | | | | |
| 720 | 9 | | | | | |
| 710 | 13 | | | 2 | | |
| 700 | 14 | 1 | | | | |
| 665–695 | | | | | | |
| 635–665 | | | 8 | 2 | | |
| 605–635 | | | 2 | | | |
| 575–605 | | | 6 | | 13 | 3 |
| 545–575 | | | 8 | | 12 | 3 |
| 515–545 | | | 9 | 1 | 15 | |
| 485–515 | | | 5 | | 6 | |
| 455–485 | | | 9 | | 7 | |
| 425–455 | | | 2 | | 1 | |
| 395–425 | | | 6 | | 3 | |
| 365–395 | | | 1 | | | |
| 335–365 | | | 3 | | | |
| 305–335 | | | 2 | | | |
| 275–305 | | | | | | |
| 245–275 | | | | | 1 | |
| 215–245 | | | | | | |
| (185)-215 | | | | | 1 | |

[a]By the definition of these groups they contain no SAT-M scores below 700.
[b]The TSWE score scale runs from 20(0) to only 60(0).

extent of learning depend greatly on educational opportunities available to the would-be learner. In turn, such opportunities arise from the adaptability of school systems to the varieties and levels of intellectual talent they are meant to serve. Therein lies a serious problem that can be illustrated by quoting from an article of mine which appeared in *Educational Researcher* (Stanley, 1980, p. 11): "While highly successful, SMPY's various [educationally facilitative] procedures occur only because the age-in-grade, Carnegie-unit lockstep of schools, both public and (especially) private, makes such heroic measures essential. If schools were organized differently, SMPY would not have been necessary—nor, indeed, would the present special provisions for most slow learners. In my opinion, age grading for instruction in academic school subjects has crept insidiously upon us as we have moved from tutorial instruction and the one-room schoolhouse to the current situation. It needs to be reversed. But, of course, that will not be done easily or quickly."

My proposal in the area of mathematics is for a longitudinal teaching team that spans kindergarten through the twelfth grade in a school system. Working from a mathematics learning center, the various members of this team would be responsible for meeting all the mathematics needs of all the students in the school system. The buck would stop with them. Every student would be helped to meet clearly stated, rather substantial criteria of mathematical competence. A few students would accomplish these early, perhaps by age eight; a few others would have to work hard until age eighteen or so in order to attain the minima. Some students would proceed far beyond the minimum essentials; others would stop with them and devote their efforts thereafter to other subject matter.

Much of the instruction might still be in groups, but not age-graded ones. Attaining levels of achievement instead of A, B, C grades would be stressed. All members of the longitudinal mathematics team would have to be highly competent, but some would specialize in helping slow learners and others in helping fast-moving students.

Obviously, this longitudinal-teaching-teams model could be applied to other subjects such as language arts, social studies, science, and foreign languages. There might also be art, music, drama, physical education, and social and emotional development teams. Attention to individualized differences, both within areas and across areas, would be increased vastly.

I should certainly like to see a sizable public school system pioneer this project for at least twenty-five years. Because of problems that one can readily anticipate and many that one cannot, almost certainly this would be extremely difficult. I believe strongly, however, that some such plan is our only hope for the educational future of America's youths. All else will be sorry stopgaps.

## Notes

This chapter is the sequel to two *College Board Review* articles (Stanley, 1977–78, in press) and two others (George and Solano, 1976; Solano, 1979). Along with eight volumes (Stanley, Keating, and Fox, 1974; Keating, 1976; Stanley, George, and Solano, 1977, 1978; George, Cohn, and Stanley, 1979; Fox, Brody, and Tobin, 1980; Bartkovich and George, 1980; and Benbow and Stanley, in preparation), those articles provide extensive background for understanding the genesis of the three groups at Johns Hopkins that search for intellectual talent, study the talented found, and try to facilitate them educationally. Those groups are as follows: the Study of Mathematically Precocious Youth (SMPY), headed by Julian C. Stanley; the Intellectually Gifted Child Study Group (IGCSG), headed by Lynn H. Fox; and the Office of Talent Identification and Development, co-directed by William C. George (for talent identification) and William G. Durden (for educational facilitation).

1. The five *Genetic Studies of Genius* volumes are Terman and others (1925); Cox (1926); Burks, Jensen, and Terman (1930); and Terman and Oden (1947, 1959). Oden (1968) is, in effect, the sixth volume of that series.

2. Duke's Talent Identification Program (TIP) is directed by Robert N. Sawyer, West Duke Building, Duke University, Durham, N.C. 27708. Arizona State's Project for the Study of Academic Precocity (PSAT) is directed by Sanford J. Cohn, Department of Special Education, Arizona State University, Tempe, Ariz. 85281.

3. Thomas Gray, "Elegy Written in a Country Churchyard," 1751, line 53.

4. The Japanese-background girl scored 760M but only 310V, the latter presumably because she had lived in the United States only a short while before taking the SAT. The Guatemalan boy readily scored 730M after being in the United States just a few months, but knew far too little English to try SAT-V or TSWE.

## References

Bartkovich, K. G., and George, W: C. *Teaching the Gifted and Talented in the Mathematics Classroom.* Washington, D.C.: National Education Association, 1980.

Benbow, C. P. "Development of Superior Mathematical Ability During Adolescence." Unpublished doctoral dissertation, Johns Hopkins University, 1981.

Benbow, C. P., and Stanley, J. C. "Sex Differences in Mathematical Ability: Fact or Artifact?" *Science,* 1980, *210* (4475, Dec. 12), 1262–1264.

Benbow, C. P., and Stanley, J. C. "Mathematical Ability: Is Sex a Factor?" *Science,* 1981, *212* (4491, Apr. 10), 118–119. Response to seven letters, published on pp. 114–118, concerning Benbow and Stanley (1980).

Benbow, C. P., and Stanley, J. C. (Eds.). *Academic Precocity: Concerning Its Development, Consequences, and Nurturance.* Johns Hopkins University. In preparation.

Burks, B. S., Jensen, D. W., and Terman, L. M. "The Promise of Youth: Follow-Up Studies of a Thousand Gifted Children." In L. M. Terman (Ed.), *Genetic Studies of Genius.* Vol. 3. Stanford, Calif.: Stanford University Press, 1930.

Cox, C. M. "The Early Mental Traits of Three Hundred Geniuses." In L. M. Terman (Ed.), *Genetic Studies of Genius.* Vol. 2. Stanford, Calif.: Stanford University Press, 1926.

Fox, L. H., Brody, L., and Tobin, D. (Eds.). *Women and the Mathematical Mystique.* Baltimore, Md.: Johns Hopkins University Press, 1980.

Galton, F. *Hereditary Genius.* London: Macmillan, 1869.

George, W. C., Cohn, S. J., and Stanley, J. C. (Eds.). *Educating the Gifted: Acceleration and Enrichment.* Baltimore, Md.: Johns Hopkins University Press, 1979.

George, W. C., and Solano, C. H. "Identifying Mathematical Talent on a Statewide Basis." In D. P. Keating (Ed.), *Intellectual Talent: Research and Development.* Baltimore, Md.: Johns Hopkins University Press, 1976.

Hobson, J. R. "High School Performance of Underage Pupils Initially Admitted to Kindergarten on the Basis of Physical and Psychological Examinations." *Educational and Psychological Measurement,* 1963, *23* (1), 159–170.

Hollingworth, L. S. *Children over 180 I.Q., Stanford-Binet.* New York: World Book Co., 1942.

Kearney, E. I., and Brockie, J. S. "Educating Gifted Children in California." In J. C. Stanley, W. C. George, and C. H. Solano (Eds.), *Educational Programs and Intellectual Prodigies.* Baltimore, Md.: Study of Mathematically Precocious Youth, Department of Psychology, Johns Hopkins University, 1978.

Keating, D. P. (Ed.). *Intellectual Talent: Research and Development.* Baltimore, Md.: Johns Hopkins University Press, 1976.

Oden, M. H. "The Fulfillment of Promise: 40-Year Follow-Up of the Terman Gifted Group." *Genetic Psychology Monographs,* 1968, *77* (1), 3–93.

Pressey, S. L. "Educational Acceleration: Appraisal and Basic Problems." *Bureau of Educational Research Monograph,* No. 31. Columbus: Ohio State University, 1949.

Sears, P. S., and Barbee, A. H. "Career and Life Satisfactions Among Terman's Gifted Women." In J. C. Stanley, W. C. George, and C. H. Solano (Eds.), *The Gifted and the Creative: A Fifty-Year Perspective.* Baltimore, Md.: Johns Hopkins University Press, 1977.

Sears, R. R. "Sources of Life Satisfactions of the Terman Gifted Men." *American Psychologist,* 1977, *32* (2), 119–128.

Solano, C. H. "The First D: Discovery of Talent, or Needles in a Haystack: Identifying the Mathematically Gifted Child." In N. Colangelo and R. T. Zaffrann (Eds.), *New Voices in Counseling the Gifted.* Dubuque, Iowa: Kendall/Hunt, 1979.

Stanley, J. C. "Test Better Finder of Great Math Talent Than Teachers Are." *American Psychologist,* 1976, *31* (4), 313–314.

Stanley, J. C. "Rationale of the Study of Mathematically Precocious Youth (SMPY) During Its First Five Years of Promoting Educational Acceleration." In J. C. Stanley, W. C. George, and C. H. Solano (Eds.), *The Gifted and the Creative: A Fifty-Year Perspective.* Baltimore, Md.: Johns Hopkins University Press, 1977.

Stanley, J. C. "The Predictive Value of the SAT for Brilliant Seventh and Eighth Graders." *College Board Review,* 1977–78, Winter (106), 30–37.

Stanley, J. C. "On Educating the Gifted." *Educational Researcher,* 1980, *9* (3), 8–12.

Stanley, J. C., and Benbow, C. P. "Using the SAT to Find Intellectually Talented Seventh Graders: A Progress Report on the Johns Hopkins University Program." *College Board Review,* in press.

Stanley, J. C., George, W. C., and Solano, C. H. (Eds.). *The Gifted and the Creative: A Fifty-Year Perspective.* Baltimore, Md.: Johns Hopkins University Press, 1977.

Stanley, J. C., George, W. C., and Solano, C. H. (Eds.) *Educational Programs and Intellectual Prodigies.* Baltimore, Md.: Study of Mathematically Precocious Youth, Department of Psychology, Johns Hopkins University, 1978.

Stanley, J. C., Keating, D. P., and Fox, L. H. (Eds.). *Mathematical Talent: Discovery, Description, and Development.* Baltimore, Md.: Johns Hopkins University Press, 1974.

Terman, L. M., and others. In L. M. Terman (Ed.), "Mental and Physical Traits of a Thousand Gifted Children." In *Genetic Studies of Genius.* Vol. 1. Stanford, Calif.: Stanford University Press, 1925.

Terman, L. M., and Oden, M. H. "The Gifted Child Grows Up: Twenty-Five Years' Follow-Up of a Superior Group." In L. M. Terman (Ed.), *Genetic Studies of Genius*. Vol. 4. Stanford, Calif.: Stanford University Press, 1947.

Terman, L. M., and Oden, M. H. "The Gifted Group at Mid-Life: Thirty-Five Years' Follow-up of the Superior Child." In L. M. Terman (Ed.), *Genetic Studies of Genius*. Vol. 5. Stanford, Calif.: Stanford University Press, 1959.

Worcester, D. A. *The Education of Children of Above-Average Mentality*. Lincoln: University of Nebraska Press, 1956.

*Julian C. Stanley is professor of psychology and director,*
*Study of Mathematically Precocious Youth (SMPY),*
*Johns Hopkins University.*

*Psychological research on imaginative response offers
a sound basis for designing tests and educational
activities for prospective artists.*

# Images—The Universal Language

*Frank Barron*

My topic is the image, whether as a physical likeness in one or more
of the sensory modalities or as a word or set of words evocative
of a physical image through memory. I am therefore using the
term *language* in a sense broader than its primary dictionary definition,
that is, as a body of words, and systems for their use, common to a
people of the same nation, community, or geographical area. Language,
in the sense in which I am using it, is "any system of formalized symbols,
signs, gestures or the like, used or conceived as a means of communicat-
ing thought or emotion."

Images as the stuff of universal language may be expressed in
words, the words serving then to evoke an image, whether abstract and
general or quite concrete and particular. I shall shortly provide some
homely examples, so we need not fret too much over these definitional
distinctions, though I find them necessary for the sake of clarity in the
argument I shall try to develop. My thesis, briefly, is that education in
school is too neglectful of the very rich resources of universal human
imagination in the students whose keeping is given to it for so many
years. And a step beyond the argument is the practical need that brings all
of us together, the need for tests of scholastic aptitude that reflect not only
currently regnant curricula but also those we can imagine just around the

W. Schrader (Ed.). *New Directions for Testing and Measurement: Measurement,
Guidance, and Program Improvement,* no. 13. San Francisco: Jossey-Bass, March 1982.

corner as we rush, or, in the case of some of us, myself included, are pushed into the electronic information and problem-solving age.

## A Sign of the Times

One evening some two years ago, I had a lot of fun watching a few hundred Standard Oil Company stockholders milling around a novel exhibit, sponsored by Chevron USA, at its unveiling in the San Francisco Museum of Science. They had been attending a stockholders meeting all day, and this was a gala champagne party to let them see a praiseworthy public service that a few of their dollars were going toward. The exhibit was titled "Creativity: The Human Resource," destined to show at many museums and popular culture centers throughout the country for the next three years.

But that is not the story; the story is in the image, the scene at opening night of the Creativity exhibit. Imagine, if you will, a huddle of burly, well-tended lads in their fifties and sixties surrounding a video-display terminal, with the usual typewriter keyboard and television screen. All eyes are on the screen, and the lads are rooting for someone and are shouting advice and even making bets. What is happening? What is on the screen? A football game? A boxing match? No, it is a game, and it is not Star Wars. The machine is talking to the player and is saying things like, "What would happen if the world's supply of gas and oil were suddenly exhausted?" or "What image can you think of that would be like an icicle melting in a bank vault?" or "like a Dow-Jones report written in invisible ink?"

Well, my memory may play me false as to the actual items in these tests of divergent thinking, but I remember the player very clearly. The player was my eleven-year-old daughter, Anthea, and the scene was to be duplicated many times that night with other children playing computer games and other stockholders watching animatedly and finally trying the games themselves. Children visiting that exhibit are always first in line— because it's fun, it's new, and they're not afraid. They're not afraid in part because they have nothing to lose, no social role and no bankroll, and in part because visual displays on a television screen that can be changed by pushing a button or twirling a knob are what they grew up with.

The examples I've given are, I must acknowledge, *about words* and *in words,* as befits my age and station in life, but the exhibit, let me hasten to add, depended heavily on visual *images:* in a film titled "The Creative Climate"; in filmed, television-type interviews with outstandingly creative, contemporary Americans; in capsule, glass-enclosed demonstrations and showings of their inventions, sculptures, compositions, and discoveries; and with many of these elements of the exhibit under some degree of control of the visitor, that is, capable of being turned on or turned off by the individual viewer occupying, as Anthea did, her own space, though with lots of people in line waiting to try.

To answer the first question that may well be in your mind, *No, I am not a Standard Oil stockholder*, and to answer your next question, *Yes, I did have a hand in designing the exhibit* and am mighty proud of it. Some four million girls and boys of all ages have since that night spent at least an hour playing and learning about "Creativity: The Human Resource" in the setting I've described, and our systematic evaluations have shown it to be an unqualified success as an adjunct to education in the schools in the cities in which it's played. I repeat *played*, for it is an entertainment compounded of images, personal and universal, and of invitations and challenges to make your own effects, to use your own imagination, and to get acquainted with images of other persons who got famous and who helped us all *by being creative.*

Now, back to my argument: that we need to make more use of images and imagistic language in our schools and to recognize and measure such image-linguistic aptitudes. That such aptitudes are distinctly different from the purely verbal, I think has been shown by the past generation of factor analytic research on the structure of intellect (Guilford, 1967); that verbal intelligence and creativity must be distinguished carefully is evident from voluminous recent research reviewed in Barron and Harrington (1981).

Indeed, the word *image* usually means something visual, as its primary dictionary definition attests (although, as I have noted, images may, of course, occur in any sensory modality). *Visual* images are what most command our attention when we sleep and dream; this is evidence enough of their preeminence and their rudimentary importance in our experience. Dreaming is one of those wonderful experiments, like twinning, that nature has so graciously performed for us psychologists. For certainly no more poised comparison of conditions for systematic observation of thought *with words* and *without words* could be, if you please, imagined; voluntary meditation and trance are experiments and practices modeled upon the dream. The dream, like silent movies without subtitles, is visual and is free of the restraint and tyranny of words. What did the movies lose when they gained the power of speech? They lost the dream, the revelry of images ungoverned by discursive rationality, and that diminished their universality and at least one sort of freedom of communication.

Proper schooling hardly ever includes provision for dreaming, though of course dreaming both awake and asleep will occur in classrooms and lecture halls, whether part of the instructional program or not. But the materials of instruction are usually audiovisual, and only in the purest of visual arts do we find programs aimed at education in images without words, and the production of images exclusively in the realm in which they most abound, the purely visual.

Tests of scholastic aptitude quite properly and realistically reflect the prevailing scholastic program, that is, life in a schoolroom and library. The studio arts wax and wane as other budgets do in the world of school, but the visual image in the living room, in the playpen, on the radar screen, along optical fibers to carry information, and graphically in the latest family of computers, looms ever larger. Two wholly new visual images do, in fact, engross us and dominate our collective conscious or unconscious memories in this generation: the mushroom cloud of the first atomic bomb blast and the unearthly beauty of Earth seen from beyond its gravitational field. These potent visual images tell us of our newness in the world: We are living in an era in which apparent natural limits have been passed. The question has become, for all of us, What are the real limits of man? and for us as educators, What are the limits of educability? How is our situation to be imagined and the images managed? (For further discussion of this, see Barron, 1979b.)

Having posed such a large question, let me turn to some modest means for measuring individual differences in the human capacity for imagination, as well as the discovering of the most powerful human means for universal, panlinguistic means of communication. Let me try to be concrete in the way one must be as a maker of psychological tests.

**Some Roads Not Taken**

Back in 1949, when I was the first research assistant at the new Institute of Personality Assessment and Research (IPAR), I had the pleasure, and educational experience, of going to the movies with Walt Disney. It happened this way. I was working at the time on some materials for what came to be known as the Barron-Welsh Figure Preference Art Scale. I knew that the scale items, figures drawn in black ink on 3 x 5-inch white cards, could be classified by factor analysis into two groups when intercorrelations were computed among them based on whether they were *liked* or *disliked* by people in general. One group of figures consisted of relatively simple, uncluttered, obviously symmetrical line drawings (circle, triangle, square, symmetrical squiggles, and so on) while the other consisted mostly of more complex and less obviously balanced figures, ranging from the merely asymmetrical to an almost cluttered complexity or even chaos. I don't intend to review here the sometimes rather muddled history of the Barron-Welsh Art Scale, but to tell you of a road not taken in the measurement of relative preference for complexity-simplicity and symmetry-asymmetry in visual displays—a road not taken then, but still open. Walt Disney and I went to the movies together because I had gone to see him about an idea I had for using animation in the creation of a series of changing abstract visual displays that would vary continuously from simple to complex, from symmetrical to asymmetrical. We were summoned from our conversation about this by Kenneth McGowan, who wanted us to sit down with some other people interested in film to watch some student-made movies at UCLA. Disney was interested, but when he mentioned the production figure in dollars for a ten-minute animation of the sort I wanted, it was I who lost interest in my previous idea. After all, the Barron-Welsh Art Scale had been produced for about $50, the Barron Picture Preference Test for $20, and even the Barron Human Movement Threshold Inkblots for only $300. There would be *no* Barron Animated Complexity Cartoon for $50,000, an opinion that was confirmed for me by Donald W. MacKinnon, director of the Institute, when I hitchhiked back to Berkeley and broke the news to him.

Yet the idea was a good one, and if, as I still think, the dimensions of complexity-simplicity and symmetry-asymmetry are not only universals in the forms of the world and archetypes of human experience but are also important gradients of perceptual synthesizing abilities, their measurement in this whole domain should be resumed and renewed. The rest of my idea at that time had been to use a theater for mass testing, perhaps with special seats to measure postural tension and fidgeting and with a panel of buttons through which the viewer could express degrees of pleasure or displeasure that would be recorded as a time series to be analyzed against the changing stimulus. Qualifiers in the form of stimuli in other sensory modalities could be introduced for purposes of experimental variation. Obviously, a host of basic questions in perception and cognition could be opened up by such an approach.

This road was not to be taken, however, as were not a number of others suggested by our work at that time. By concentrating on the social outcome we called creativity, which is a mixture of ability, achievement, luck, motive, and means for attaining fame, we at IPAR engaged in research with some very interesting social and educational problems, but at a cost of energy that might have been devoted to basic research. I know that I can safely confide this to members of the Educational Testing Service, dedicated as it is to the promotion of positive and practical social outcomes.

### Inkblots, Imagination, and Empathy

Perhaps the granddaddy of all stimuli for the testing of imagination is the glob. A glob is something like a blob, which is akin to a bubble—a drop, splotch, daub, or small, rounded lump of some plastic, malleable, moldable substance. A glob is a sort of globular blob or daub. Clouds and inkblots and drops of oil on water are ideal invitations to imagination to make something of them. They are before language, for sure, rudimentary indefinite images, the stuff of creation. Max Ernst liked rubbing as a way to bring out the hidden form in substances, and his essay, "Inspiration to Order," a wonderfully ambiguous title, proclaimed frottage and collage as sacred exercises in that early Dada manifesto, with its concluding chuckle, "For DaDa comes with a smile on its lips to destroy the past." The unformed, or only vaguely formed, is a challenge to the creator. Binet saw this and played Rorschach long before Rorschach did, and, of course, so did Galton, and Wilhelm Stern, and Wertheimer, and even Wundt. Out of the glob comes "good form." The process of change is from diffusion to integration, from chaos to order, and perhaps back again.

So what does all that have to do with the measurement of imaginative capacity? To put it bluntly, Rorschach was on the right track, or road, but he got flagged down too soon. My own efforts to provide more refined measures for the radical Rorschach hypotheses went no further than my Threshold for Human Movement (M) scale, a set of 26 inkblots chosen from an initial item pool of 150 inkblots to form a series with M-evocative powers, defined as frequency of elicitation of an M-response, ranging from .00 to 1.00 through graduations of .04. I put forward, in my standardization article, the idea of using that model to creative threshold measures for W (the tendency to offer an interpretation encompassing the whole), for form, for color, for form-color dominance, and for originality or adaptive response to the demand for irreality. The farthest I got with my own ideas was to develop a multiple choice human movement series offering opportunities for alternative interpretations of each blot as human, animal, or inanimate movement, pure form, and originality in pure form versus originality in human movement. Once again, note how enhanced such an approach might be with the use of modern computer graphic techniques for composition, display, and interpretation of ambiguous and improbable, in varying specifiable degrees, forms.

**Symbolic Equivalence**

Let me turn now to the measurement of individual differences in the ability to recognize equivalences of form, of a sort that might be called symbolic equivalence or gestalt equivalence, as well as the ability to generate equivalent (or *transposed, transformed)* gestalts. D'Arcy W. Thompson's *On Growth and Form*, by mathematizing organic morphology, has accustomed us to think of this as the mechanism of organic evolution, or the creative process in nature *par excellence*. J. P. Guilford, in his "Structure of Intellect" model, has a place for "the transformation of the systems" in the various contents he recognizes, from semantic to behavioral. It is this sort of ability and process I have in mind when I speak of the ability to recognize and to generate (produce) symbolic equivalences. (For a discussion of this, see "The Transformation of Systems of Images," in Barron, 1979b, pp. 250–255.)

Here a "test example" from the Barron Symbol Equivalence Test may suffice to give the general idea. The test respondent is given the task to "think of metaphors or similis or more-or-less equivalent images" for certain given (stimulus) images. One example is: "a civilian population fleeing chaotically before armed invaders," "handkerchiefs seen through the window of a Bendix dryer," and "chips of wood borne downstream by a swiftly eddying current." The wording of the instructions and the examples may be varied according to the age and education of the respondents. College students, for example, take well to Shelley's images, "O wild west wind, thou breath of Autumn's being" and "the leaves dead, like ghosts from an enchanter fleeing." The test has shown very substantial validities against external criteria of creativity (real-life performance as judged or rated) in a variety of samples, of both sexes, ranging in age from seven to seventy (Barron, 1972, 1974, 1977; Chambers and Barron, 1978).

## The San Francisco Art Institute Study

Note that now I am speaking of images expressed in words. Such a task could be of great theoretical interest in these days of academic infatuation with differentiation of function in the left and right hemispheres of the brain, but I confess to ignorance on this subject, which entitles me to be silent. But anyone may note that art nowadays is often conceptual and most of its meaning can be expressed in words, and poetry is increasingly imagistic and wars against verbal abstraction. Both painters and poets use words and visual images prominently in their work. I am far from arguing for a concentration on images to the exclusion of words. In my creativity workshops at the University of California, Santa Cruz, I use visual displays—the Child Esthetic Judgment Test, for example—to stimulate discussion of the images and their power, and also, following the prototype of the William Carlos Williams poems on Breugel's paintings, as an occasion for verbal description and for the writing of poetry.

My own systematic research with art students supports the notion that tests calling for imagination are the best predictors of ability in art. Let me take as example one such study, which is particularly relevant to the ETS program in the arts, emphasizing as it does the ratings of portfolios as well as criteria of performance based on grade-point average in studio courses, and including a detailed look at the predictive efficiency of tests.

*Research Design and Methods.* The basic design of this prediction study at the San Francisco Art Institute was as follows: (1) obtain portfolios of recent work from entering freshmen and rate them for artistic potential; (2) test entering freshmen with a battery of psychological tests, including performance measures as well as questionnaires; (3) correlate tests with portfolios; (4) correlate tests with grades at end of first year; (5) obtain new portfolios of work completed by end of first year and relate ratings of these first-year portfolios to test results; (6) continue to gather information such as grades and exhibits of work throughout the four-year course leading to the bachelor of fine arts degree; and (7) obtain final criterion information in the form of faculty ratings, peer ratings, grade-point average, honors, and scholarship support and out of this construct a composite criterion for prediction. If possible, repeat the study on a second class.

The study was completed more or less as planned. We did discuss carrying the study to completion, and we did test a second class, with a reduced battery of tests, to check out results from the first. The research involved many things besides prediction of student performance, of course, and much of the data have already been reported in *Artists in the Making* (Barron, 1972), which contains a full description of the test battery and gives basic statistics descriptive of the student samples and of interrelationships among variables. The initial interview study has also been reported there. My concern here is to give an overview of the prediction study, with particular attention to the role of imagery, its discrimination and its genesis, in artistic creativity. The test battery included such measures as these:

- Adjective Self-Description
- Artist Self-Rating on Creativity
- Barron-Welsh Art Scale
- Barron M-Threshold Inkblots
- Child Esthetic Preference Test
- Consequences Test, Parts I and II
- Franck Drawing Completion Test
- Gottschaldt Figures Test
- Hardyck Stick Figures
- Mosaic Judgment Test
- Perceptual Acuity Test
- Symbol Equivalence Test, Parts I and II

In addition, the Juhasz Sensory Reasoning Test was administered individually to twenty-five of these students.

*The Entering Portfolio Study.* Although all ninety-one entering students were required to submit portfolios, only forty-eight complied. (This large-scale ignoring of requests to submit work for comparative evaluation held true also when similar requests emanating from the dean of student's office were made at year's end for both classes. Many students viewed it as an imposition when asked to bring in their work for evaluation, in some cases considering it immoral and in other cases just a demand too inconveniencing to be met.)

The forty-eight student portfolios at entrance were rated by eight senior faculty members of the Art Institute and by four of my staff members, including the principal investigator and the director of the testing project. Ratings were based on a three-step classification in terms of "degree to which the student has potential for serious work in art." The eight Art Institute faculty members' ratings were then averaged and correlated with the averaged ratings of the four staff members; a correlation of .50 results. Further analysis by sex of students showed an interesting difference, however; the two staffs, art faculty and psychological researchers, correlate .67 with one another when males are rated, but only .01 when females are rated. The details of this finding are given in the following table.

**Table 1. Correlations of San Francisco Art Institute and Psychologist Raters on SFAI Student Portfolios**

|  | N | Male | N | Female | N | Total |
|---|---|---|---|---|---|---|
| Tested students in sample | 32 | .666 | 16 | .008 | 48 | .499 |
| Tested students, including some not in sample | 33 | .669 | 18 | -.014 | 51 | .496 |
| All students rated, including some not tested | 40 | .611 | 22 | .264 | 62 | .501 |

Informal conversations between the principal investigator and the Art Institute faculty raters explored attitudes towards male versus female students on the part of the faculty, which as it happens is all male. These conversations left the principal investigator with a very strong impression that female art students are not taken very seriously by the faculty. Typical comments: "They may hang on and graduate, but then all they ever do is teach school or get married and get a job in something else"; "They *never* have a one-man show—never, not one in the whole history of the school." Support for this view of sex differences in professional success so far as art is concerned may be found in interviews with the most promising of the female students, as reported in *Artists in the Making* (Barron, 1972, chaps. 1–3).

Correlations of test results with the portfolio ratings revealed still other differences in what the raters seem to be responding to. These may be summarized as follows:

1. Portfolio ratings by the Art Institute faculty raters proved to be significantly correlated with a number of self-ratings and interests or attitude scales, but unrelated to all but one of the performance and

esthetic judgment tests. The single exception in the performance domain is the Human Movement tendency on the Inkblot Form Test (a positive correlation of .28).

2. The psychologist staff's ratings of portfolios produced an entirely different set of correlations, being positively associated only with performance on the Perceptual Acuity Test and the Gottschaldt Figures. These are measures of accuracy of perception and analytic powers rather than transformation of images.

3. As indicated earlier, there were sex differences observable in the ratings. The psychologists' ratings of portfolios for the female students alone correlated quite highly with their scores on the Child Test of Esthetic Judgment. The SFAI faculty ratings for female students had a high negative correlation with the Barron-Welsh Art Scale.

*Grade-Point Average.* A correlational analysis of all tests against the total grade-point average at the end of three semesters was carried out. Quite sensible correlations (at the .01 level) with the criterion appear in that analysis:

1. Self-ratings

   The highest correlations in self-ratings are:

   | | |
   |---|---|
   | When compared to the work of other students at my level, my work is unusually creative. | .62 |
   | I work spontaneously rather than deliberately. | .60 |
   | I have definite feelings about most art work I see. | .58 |
   | I like my own work. | .57 |

2. Performance tests

   | | |
   |---|---|
   | Symbol Equivalence, Part II (total) | .61 |
   | Consequences I (total) | .47 |
   | Inkblot Form Test, Part I: M-volume | .44 |
   | Part II: M-total | .51 |

3. Personal outlook

   | | |
   |---|---|
   | Adjective Self-description: Artist scale | .49 |
   | Complexity of outlook | .48 |

*The Composite Criterion.* This criterion consists of information from several sources, combined to yield an overall score of 3, 2, or 1 for all students on whom there was enough information to arrive at such a judgment. It should be emphasized that for most students in the sample, information was quite fragmentary. Faculty ratings and peer ratings reveal this fact rather dramatically. The average faculty rater knew only nine or ten students four years after matriculation, and the average student rater knew only a few more of his peers than the faculty did. Fortunately, there was little overlap in who was known to whom, so that a composite picture could be constructed by allowing credit for being known and highly rated by only five or six raters. Nearly 60 percent of the entering students were not remembered by *anyone* four years later, not by peers, not by faculty, not by the director, not by the dean of admissions.

At first blush, this finding looked rather damning for the institution, but a little informal research at another college among faculty and students confirmed that most members of the graduating class did not know one another, did not remember dropouts from four or three years earlier, at least by name, and were not known at all by many faculty members. Perhaps this is simply the way things are in institutions of higher learning with enrollments in the hundreds. In any event, the composite criterion was finally arrived at, with other information contributing, such as scholarship support and awards and honors (scored *plus*, of course). This final overall rating was then checked out with the admissions office, and cases on which there was any disagreement were scrutinized further. Use was made uniformly of the college transcript and faculty evaluations when they were available.

A correlation analysis reveals many significant correlations with the composite criterion, though none is as high as .50 and only a few are in the range of .40 to .50. The main significantly positive correlations are with the Gottschaldt Figures, the Consequences Test, the Symbol Equivalence Test, and the self-rating "I completely lose myself while working, forgetting all other personal matters." The self-rating "My work is unique" is also positive. Finally, a variable from the Juhasz Test purporting to measure accuracy of taste discrimination correlated positively with the composite criterion.

In the main, these correlations reflect a picture consistent with what one might expect of someone with the motivation and ability to be an artist. Basically, the more imaginative students did better work. They could break set (resist a given perceptual gestalt, as in the Gottschaldt test), think suppositionally (Consequences), generate metaphors (Symbol Equivalence), and concentrate their attention on their own imaginative processes to the exclusion of others.

**What Are the Implications for Action?**

From our general experience as well as specific results in this research program, we feel able to make several recommendations in the areas of pedagogy, identification of giftedness, student and program evaluation, and future research on theoretical issues.

*Pedagogy.* Educational efforts should be directed to devising instructional programs specifically for improvement in measurable functions found to be related to creativity and effective performance in esthetic endeavors. These include most prominently the cultivation of flexibility, complexity of perception, human empathy, esthetic judgment, metaphorical thinking, symbolic scope, and originality. The very tests that we have used to measure these functions may be used as models for the development of exercises to enhance the abilities themselves. We are thinking here not only of art curricula but also of schooling in general.

Further, we think it useful to awaken awareness in students of their own characteristic modes of expression by having samples of their work described objectively to them in terms of the variables we developed for rating works of art. We refer here to dimensions such as complexity-simplicity, symmetry-asymmetry, expansion-construction, hedonic tone, configurational and chromatic dynamism, and the relative strengths of geometry, abstraction, and representation in their expression.

***Identification of Giftedness.*** If one wants to use tests for this purpose, we recommend a small battery of tests that can be administered in a group setting and scored objectively and without specially trained or skilled personnel. In addition to the Gottschaldt Figures and the Barron-Welsh Art Scale, we would suggest the M-threshold Inkblot Form Test, the Consequences Test, and the Symbol Equivalence Test. Finally, we believe firmly in obtaining self-diagnosis and self-description as a first step in understanding a person's creativity, so we recommend something like the artist self-rating scales we employed in the study cited.

***Student and Program Evaluation.*** First of all, we recommend the use of a definite grading system that will accommodate a wide range of judgment of performance in all subjects. This is not simply for the convenience of administrators or researchers; we believe from our general experience and from our evaluation research both at the San Francisco Art Institute and at College V, University of California, Santa Cruz, that it is extremely valuable to students to receive information about their comparative performance. It is also valuable information for evaluation of the educational program itself.

We recommend also that both students and programs be evaluated through application of the same tests we have recommended for identification of talent. This may be done by repeated testing at appropriate intervals. The course of learning for individual students may thus be followed, and also the program as a whole may be evaluated for its effect on the functions measured.

***Future Research on Theoretical Issues.*** We recommend extensive cross-cultural application of several of the measures found useful in these studies, with special attention to the cross-cultural comparison of developmental norms and sex differences. Some efforts have already been made in this direction, particularly with the Gottschaldt Figures, the Child Esthetic Preference Test, the Barron-Welsh Art Scale, and the Perceptual Acuity Test. Many of the tests were employed in our twin studies in Italy, but what we are recommending here is systematic measurement in a wide variety of cultures and in a wide age range.

The twin method should be developed further by refining the measurement of environmental and educational influences. We have already, as reported in *Artists in the Making,* established a substantial genetic basis for artistic aptitudes; this should be followed by educational experiments in which one member of an identical twin pair is given special training of the sort described in our pedagogical recommendations, so that a precise measure of educability might be obtained by comparing later performance of the experimental twin with the co-twin control. This should be done with twins in a wide age range, so that something might be learned about proper timing of educational experiences for maximum effect.

Finally, we recommend more detailed longitudinal study of individual artists of high ability. We have deliberately adopted a measurement approach primarily in the present research, but we believe that it can be combined with a personological approach through study of the entire life span of creative, artistic individuals. The motivation to create is of central importance, and it can best be understood by understanding its workings in the lives of individuals.

## References

Barron, F. *Artists in the Making.* New York: Seminar Press, 1972.

Barron, F. *Basic Research in Esthetic Education.* Washington, D.C.: U.S. Office of Education, 1974.

Barron, F. "Symbolic Scope as a Predictor of Ability in Art." In S. L. Carmean and B. L. Grover (Eds.), *Creative Thinking.* Eighth Western Symposium on Learning. Bellingham: Western Washington University, 1977.

Barron, F. "Educability at the Upper Limits of Performance Potential." Paper presented at meeting of the American Association for the Advancement of Science, Houston, January 1979a.

Barron, F. *The Shaping of Personality.* New York: Harper & Row, 1979b.

Barron, F., and Harrington, D. "Creativity, Intelligence, and Personality." In M. R. Rosenzweig and L. W. Porter (Eds.), *Annual Review of Psychology.* Vol. 32. Palo Alto, Calif.: Annual Reviews, 1981.

Chambers, J.A.A., and Barron, F. *Identifying the Culturally Different Gifted Student.* Final report under grant no. 77-11-D. Sacramento: California State Department of Education, 1978.

Guilford, J. P. *The Nature of Human Intelligence.* New York: McGraw-Hill, 1967.

Thompson, D. W. *On Growth and Form.* Cambridge, England: Cambridge University Press, 1917.

*Frank Barron is professor of psychology, University of California, Santa Cruz.*

# Index